WAKING *the* DEAD

WAKING *the* DEAD

THE GLORY OF A HEART FULLY ALIVE

JOHN ELDREDGE

THOMAS NELSON PUBLISHERS®
Nashville

A Division of Thomas Nelson, Inc.
www.ThomasNelson.com

Published in Nashville, Tennessee, by Thomas Nelson, Inc.

Published in association with Yates & Yates, LLP, Attorneys and Counselors, Orange, California.

Unless otherwise noted, Scripture quotations are from the HOLY BIBLE: NEW INTERNATIONAL VERSION®. Copyright © 1973, 1978, 1984 by International Bible Society. Used by permission of Zondervan Publishing House. All rights reserved.

Scripture quotations noted NLT are from the *Holy Bible,* New Living Translation, copyright © 1996. Used by permission of Tyndale House Publishers, Inc., Wheaton, Illinois 60189. All rights reserved.

Scripture quotations noted NKJV are from THE NEW KING JAMES VERSION. Copyright © 1979, 1980, 1982, Thomas Nelson, Inc., Publishers.

Scripture quotations noted *The Message* are from *The Message: The New Testament in Contemporary English.* Copyright © 1993 by Eugene H. Peterson.

Scripture quotations noted NRSV are from THE NEW REVISED STANDARD VERSION of the Bible. Copyright © 1989 by the Division of Christian Education of the National Council of the Churches of Christ in the U.S.A. All rights reserved.

Scripture quotations noted NASB are from the NEW AMERICAN STANDARD BIBLE®, Copyright © The Lockman Foundation 1960, 1962, 1963, 1968, 1971, 1972, 1973, 1975, 1977, 1995. Used by permission. (www.Lockman.org)

Scripture quotations noted KJV are from the KING JAMES VERSION.

Scripture quotations noted *Moffatt* are from *The Bible: James Moffatt Translation* by James A. R. Moffatt. Copyright © 1950, 1952, 1953, 1954, by James A. R. Moffatt.

Library of Congress Cataloging-in-Publication Data

Eldredge, John.
  Waking the dead: the glory of a heart fully alive / John Eldredge.
    p. cm.
  Includes bibliographical references.
  ISBN 0-7852-6553-8 (hardcover)
  1. Christian life. I. Title.
BV4501.3.E43 2003
248.4—dc21   2003006570

Printed in the United States of America
04 05 06 07 BVG 5

The glory of God is man fully alive.

—SAINT IRENAEUS

CONTENTS

PART 1: SEEING OUR WAY CLEARLY

Chapter One: Arm Yourselves   3

Chapter Two: The Eyes of the Heart   19

Chapter Three: The Heart of All Things   36

PART 2: THE RANSOMED HEART

Chapter Four: Ransomed and Restored   55

Chapter Five: The Glory Hidden in Your Heart   71

PART 3: THE FOUR STREAMS

Chapter Six: Walking with God   91

Chapter Seven: Receiving God's Intimate Counsel   110

Chapter Eight: Deep Restoration   128

Chapter Nine: Spiritual Warfare: Fighting for Your Heart   147

Chapter Ten: Setting Hearts Free: 164
                Integrating the Four Streams

PART 4: THE WAY OF THE HEART

Chapter Eleven: Fellowships of the Heart   185

Chapter Twelve: Like the Treasures of the Kingdom   204

Appendix: A Daily Prayer for Freedom   223

Acknowledgments   227

Excerpt from The Journey of Desire   228

About the Author   244

PART ONE

SEEING OUR WAY CLEARLY

The way through the world
Is more difficult to find than the way beyond it.

—WALLACE STEVENS

Narrow the road that leads to life, and only a few find it.

—JESUS OF NAZARETH (MATT. 7:14)

There are few things more crucial to us than our own lives.

And there are few things we are less clear about.

This journey we are taking is hardly down the yellow brick road. Then again, that's not a bad analogy at all. We may set out in the light, with hope and joy, but eventually, our path always seems to lead us into the woods, shrouded with a low-lying mist. Where is this abundant life that Christ supposedly promised? Where is God when we need him most? What is to become of us?

The cumulative effect of days upon years that we do not really understand is a subtle *erosion*. We come to doubt our place, we come to question God's intentions toward us, and we lose track of the most important things in life.

We're not fully convinced that God's offer to us *is* life. We have forgotten that the heart is central. And we had no idea that we were born into a world at war.

CHAPTER ONE

ARM YOURSELVES

The thief comes only to steal and kill and destroy;
I have come that they may have life, and have it to the full.

—JESUS OF NAZARETH (JOHN 10:10)

We and the world, my children, will always be at war.
Retreat is impossible.
Arm yourselves.

—LEIF ENGER

We were running low on fuel, and still the fog refused to lift. Icy Straight spread out below us, beautiful and threatening. I've always loved the ocean, the wilder the better. But clearly, this was no place to run out of gas. If by chance we survived ditching the small plane, we'd last about seven minutes in those waters. The nearest chance at rescue lived more than forty minutes away. *Great. This is just how it happens,* I thought. *We'll make* Reader's Digest. *"Family on vacation lost in fatal crash."* Rain and mist smeared the windshield as we strained our eyes ahead, searching for a break in the clouds. There's no radar in these planes; bush pilots fly VFR—visual flight rules. If you can't see where you're going, well, then, mister, you can't go there. And you can't keep trying forever, either; the clock that's running is the fuel gauge. Three more minutes, and we'll have to turn back.

"We'll give it one more pass."

"Fairweather Mountain" is a total misnomer. With a name like that, don't you picture some lovely place in Hawaii or maybe Costa Rica—balmy breezes, gentle green slopes, the weather always, well, *fair*? These mountains explode 15,000 feet or more above sea level, right off the coast of southeastern Alaska, sheer cliffs and foreboding glaciers. Some of the world's worst weather hangs out here.

The pilot was yelling above the drone of the engine, "They get their name 'cause you can only see 'em in fair weather."

How cute. What idiot came up with that cleverness? Raw fear had swallowed my sense of humor whole. *They ought to have named them the Peaks of Frozen Death or the Don't Even Think About It Mountains.* Fair weather? Around here, that means maybe twenty days a year—if you're lucky.

We got lucky.

And I have never seen anything more breathtaking in all my life. We banked along vertical granite walls that rose and fell thousands of feet on either side, like a sparrow gliding among the Himalayas. "Are those waterfalls?" I asked, pointing to several cascades of white falling through thin air over the black cliffs.

"Avalanches. It must be warm up here today."

Massive crevasses in the glaciers below held pools of clear water—a color I never knew existed, something between azure and cerulean blue.

"Those cracks are so big we could fly right down 'em."

I pretended not to hear. I felt we'd slipped through Death's grasp, and I didn't want to give him another swipe. The beauty that now engulfed us was enough.

IN DESPERATE NEED OF CLARITY

Twenty clear days a year—that sounds about like my life. I think I see what's really going on about that often. The rest of the time, it feels like fog, like the bathroom mirror after a hot shower. You know what I mean. What exactly are you perfectly clear on these days? How about your life? Why have things gone the way they have? Where was God in all that? And do you know what you ought to do next, with a deep, settled confidence that it will work out? Neither do I. Oh, I'd *love* to wake each morning knowing exactly who I am and where God is taking me. Zeroed in on all my relationships, undaunted in my calling. It's awesome when I do see. But for most of us, life seems more like driving along with a dirty windshield and then turning into the sun. I can sort of make out the shapes ahead, and I think the light is green.

Wouldn't a little bit of clarity go a long way right now?

Let's start with why life is so dang *hard*. You try to lose a little weight, but it never seems to happen. You think of making a shift in your career, maybe even serving God, but you never actually get to it. Perhaps a few of you do make the jump, but it rarely pans out the way you thought. You try to recover something in your marriage, and your spouse looks at you with a glance that says, "Nice try," or "Isn't it a little late for that?" and the thing actually blows up into an argument in front of the kids. Yes, we have our faith. But even there—maybe *especially* there—it all seems to fall rather short of the promise. There's talk of freedom and abundant life, of peace like a river and joy unspeakable, but we see precious little of it, to be honest.

Why is it that, as Tillich said, it's only "here and there in the world and now and then in ourselves" we see any evidence of a new creation? Here and there, now and then. In other words . . . not much. When you stand them side by side, the *description* of the Christian life practically shouted in the New Testament compared with the *actual* life of most Christians, it's . . . embarrassing. Paul sounds like a madman, and we look a little foolish, like children who've been held back a grade. Why is it that nearly every good thing, from taking the annual family vacation to planning a wedding to cultivating a relationship, takes so much work?

It's almost as if there is something set against us.

SHELL SHOCK

Some dear friends of mine just returned from a three-week vacation in France. It had been their dream for nearly twenty-five years. What could be more romantic than strolling the Champs Élysées in the evening, as lovers do? It seemed an ideal way to celebrate their twenty-fifth wedding anniversary. They'd both served God faithfully for decades, but over the years a European rendezvous seemed about as reachable as the moon. Then, late last fall, things suddenly came together.

Friends of theirs were headed to Europe and offered two tickets to come along. Time off was available. They were going to France. And right after they made it to Paris, it all fell apart. Craig came down with walking pneumonia; Lori wanted to leave the third day. All sorts of issues in their marriage surfaced, but since they were with friends, the issues mostly played themselves out in their own thoughts—which tended toward divorce. It wasn't romantic; it was *hard*. Afterward, as we talked on the phone about the whole thing, Lori said, "Life never seems to turn out the way you think it will, about 90 percent of the time." No kidding. Haven't we all got a story that goes with that little bumper sticker?

Just the day before, I received another call. That was the morning our son Blaine was to have his final cardiologist appointment, and I was anxious to hear the news. Now, I know that every parent thinks his child is head and shoulders above the rest, but I'm telling you—Blaine is a special one. He turned eleven this year, and he's one of the healthiest, happiest kids I've ever known. His heart is so good, so spiritually aware, so keen to the hearts of others. He's surprisingly compassionate for a boy his age, and he's also the most courageous one of us all. When it comes to rock climbing or cliff jumping or skiing, Blaine is always the first to go for it. He's a great athlete and a talented artist and a riot when it comes to his humor. He plays the violin; he memorizes cowboy poetry; he blows stuff up; he wants to be a Jedi knight. I love this boy.

And it's a long story of prayer and hope and worry over Blaine. When he was young, his pediatrician picked up an anomaly in his heart during a routine checkup. The cardiologist confirmed through a battery of tests that, indeed, Blaine had several holes in his heart. "He'll need surgery," he said. We opted to wait until Blaine was older, to give God a chance to intervene. The thought of putting my son under open-heart surgery gave me the shudders.

Over the course of those years we spent many nights in prayer that God would heal Blaine's heart. During one of those times, Stasi, not usually given to visions, had a picture of a light penetrating his heart. At that moment, she felt certain God had healed him. And just this morning, the day for his annual checkup, as I began to pray for Blaine, I sensed Jesus say, *I've healed him.* My heart rested, and I waited for the good report.

"Hi . . . it's me." A long silence. "Blaine needs surgery . . . right away."

Hope vanished. I felt that sick-in-the-gut feeling of an imminent free fall, that feeling you get on top of a ladder that's starting to sway under you. All kinds of thoughts and emotions rushed in. *What? Oh, no . . . Not after all this . . . I . . . I thought . . .* My heart was sinking. Despair, betrayal, abandonment by God. Failure on our part to pray enough or believe enough. I felt moments away from a total loss of heart. It seemed inevitable.

These moments aren't a rational, calculated progression of thought; they're more like being tossed out of a raft in a storm. It comes fast and furious, but the pull of the current is always toward a loss of heart. Most of the time we are swept away; we give in, lose heart, and climb out of it sometime later. Some never climb out.

EYES TO SEE

When Spillane (*The Perfect Storm*) treats injured seamen offshore, one of the first things he evaluates is their degree of consciousness. The highest level, known as "alert and oriented times four," describes almost everyone in an everyday situation. They know who they are, where they are, what time it is, and what's just happened. If someone suffers a blow to the head, the first thing they lose is recent events—"alert and oriented times three"—and the last thing they lose is their identity. A person who has lost all levels of consciousness, right down to their identity, is said to be "alert and oriented times zero." When John Spillane wakes up in the water, he is alert and oriented times zero. His understanding of the world is reduced to the fact that he exists, nothing more. Almost simultaneously, he understands that he is in excruciating pain. For a long time, that is all he knows.

John Spillane is a para-rescue jumper sent into the North Atlantic, into the worst storm of the twentieth century, the *perfect storm,* as the book and film called it, to rescue a fisherman lost at sea. When his helicopter goes down, he is forced to jump into pitch blackness from an unknown height, and when he hits the water, he's going so fast it's like hitting the pavement from eighty feet above. He is dazed and confused—just as we are when it comes to the story of our lives. It's the perfect analogy. We have no idea who we really are, why we're here, what's happened to us, or why. Honestly, most days we are alert and oriented times zero.

Has God abandoned us? Did we not pray enough? Is this just something we accept as "part of life," suck it up, even though it breaks our hearts? After a while, the accumulation of event after event that we do not like and do not understand erodes our confidence that we are part of something grand and good, and reduces us to a survivalist mind-set. I know, I know—we've been told that we matter to God. And part of us partly believes it. But life has a way of chipping away at that conviction, undermining our settled belief that he means us well. I mean, if that's true, then why didn't he _____ ? Fill in the blank. Heal your mom. Save your marriage. Get you married. Help you out more.

Either (*a*) we're blowing it, or (*b*) God is holding out on us. Or some combination of both, which is where most people land. Think about it. Isn't this where *you* land, with all the things that haven't gone the way you'd hoped and wanted? Isn't it some version of "I'm blowing it"? in that it's your fault, you could have done better, you could have been braver or wiser or more beautiful or something? Or "God is holding out on me," in that you know he *could* come through, but he hasn't come through—and what are you to make of that?

This is The Big Question, by the way, the one every philosophy and religion and denominational take on Christianity has been trying to nail down since the dawn of time. *What is really going on here?* Good grief—life is brutal. Day after day it hammers us, till we lose sight of what God intends toward us, and we haven't the foggiest idea why the things that are happening to us *are* happening to us. Then you watch lives going down with the Twin Towers, read about children starving in Ethiopia, and wham! If a good God is really in charge . . . all that.

I felt so bad that Paris wasn't what my friends hoped it would be, but I wasn't sure what to say. Like most Christians in that situation, I simply asked Lori how I could pray for them. "That we would have eyes to see what's going on." My heart leaped. Brilliant! Perfect! That is *exactly* what we need. Eyes to see. Isn't that what Jesus offered us—clarity? Recovery of sight for the blind (Luke 4:18)? We need clarity and we need it badly. A simple prayer rises from my heart: *Jesus, take away the fog and the clouds and the veil, and help me to see . . . give me eyes to really see.*

THE OFFER IS *LIFE*

The glory of God is man fully alive. (Saint Irenaeus)

When I first stumbled across this quote, my initial reaction was . . . *You're kidding me. Really?* I mean, is that what you've been told? That the purpose of God—the very thing he's staked his reputation on—is your coming fully alive? Huh. Well, that's a different take on things. It made me wonder, *What* are *God's intentions toward me? What is it I've come to believe about that?* Yes, we've been told any number of times that God does care, and there are some pretty glowing promises given to us in Scripture along those lines. But on the other hand, we have the days of our lives, and they have a way of casting a rather long shadow over our hearts when it comes to God's intentions toward *us* in particular. I read the quote again, "The glory of God is man fully alive," and something began to stir in me. *Could it be?*

I turned to the New Testament to have another look, read for myself what Jesus said he offers. "I have come that they may have life, and have it to the full" (John 10:10). Wow. That's different from saying, "I have come to forgive you. Period." Forgiveness is awesome, but Jesus says here he came to give us *life*. Hmmm. Sounds like ol' Irenaeus might be on to something. "I am the bread of life" (John 6:48). "Whoever believes in me, as the Scripture has said, streams of living water will flow from within him" (John 7:38). The more I looked, the more this whole theme of life jumped off the pages. I mean, it's *everywhere*.

Above all else, guard your heart,
> for it is the wellspring of life. (Prov. 4:23)

You have made known to me the path of life. (Ps. 16:11)

In him was life, and that life was the light of men. (John 1:4)

Come to me to have life. (John 5:40)

Tell the people the full message of this new life. (Acts 5:20)

I began to get the feeling of a man who's been robbed. I'm well aware that it's life I *need*, and it's life I'm looking for. But the offer has gotten "interpreted" by well-meaning people to say, "Oh, well. Yes, of course . . . God intends life for you. But that is *eternal* life, meaning, because of the death of Jesus Christ you can go to heaven when you die." And that's true . . . in a way. But it's like saying getting married means, "Because I've given you this ring, you will be taken care of in your retirement." And in the meantime? Isn't there a whole lot more to the relationship *in the meantime*? (It's in the meantime that we're living out our days, by the way.) Are we just lost at sea? What did Jesus mean when he promised us life? I go back to the source, and what I find is just astounding.

I am still confident of this:
> I will see the goodness of the LORD
> in the land of the living. (Ps. 27:13)

"I tell you the truth," Jesus said to them, "no one who has left home or wife or brothers or parents or children for the sake of the kingdom of God will fail to receive many times as much in this age and, in the age to come, eternal life." (Luke 18:29–30)

Jesus doesn't locate his offer to us only in some distant future after we've slogged our way through our days here on earth. He talks about a life available to us *in this age.* So does Paul: "Godliness has value for all things, holding promise for both the present life and the life to come" (1 Tim. 4:8). Our *present* life and the next. When we hear the words *eternal life,* most of us tend to interpret that as "a life that waits for us in eternity." But *eternal* means "unending," not "later." The Scriptures use the term to mean we can never lose it. It's a life that can't be taken from us. The offer is life, and that life starts *now.*

> Just as Christ was raised from the dead by the glorious power of the Father, *now* we also may live new lives. (Rom. 6:4 NLT, emphasis added)

The glory of God is man fully alive? Now? Hope unbidden rose at the thought that God's intentions toward me might be better than I'd thought. His happiness and my happiness are tied together? My coming fully alive is what he's committed to? *That's* the offer of Christianity? Wow! I mean, it would make no small difference if we knew—and I mean *really* knew—that down-deep-in-your-toes kind of knowing that no one and nothing can talk you out of—if we *knew* that our lives and God's glory were bound together. Things would start looking up. It would feel promising, like making friends on the first day of school with the biggest kid in class.

The offer is life. Make no mistake about that. So then . . . where *is* that life? Why is it so rare?

WE ARE AT WAR

> The thief comes only to steal and kill and destroy; I have come that they may have life, and have it to the full. (John 10:10)

Have you ever wondered why Jesus married those two statements? Did you even know he spoke them at the same time? I mean, he says them in one breath. And he has his reasons. By all means, God intends life for you. But right now that life is *opposed*. It doesn't just roll in on a tray. There is a thief. He comes to steal and kill and destroy. In other words, yes, the offer is life, but you're going to have to fight for it because there's an Enemy in your life with a different agenda.

There *is* something set against us.

We are at war.

How I've missed this for so long is a mystery to me. Maybe I've overlooked it; maybe I've chosen not to see. *We are at war*. I don't like that fact any more than you do, but the sooner we come to terms with it, the better hope we have of making it through to the life we do want. This is not Eden. You probably figured that out. This is not Mayberry; this is not *Seinfeld*'s world; this is not *Survivor*. The world in which we live is a combat zone, a violent clash of kingdoms, a bitter struggle unto the death. I'm sorry if I'm the one to break this news to you: you were born into a world at war, and you will live all your days in the midst of a great battle, involving all the forces of heaven and hell and played out here on earth.

Where *did* you think all this opposition was coming from?

Earlier in the Story, back in the beginning of our time on earth, a great glory was bestowed upon us. We all—men and women— were created in the image of God. Fearfully and wonderfully made, fashioned as living icons of the bravest, wisest, most stunning Person who ever lived. Those who have ever seen him fell to their knees without even thinking about it, as you find yourself breathless before the Grand Canyon or the Alps or the sea at dawn. That glory was shared with us; we were, in Chesterton's phrase, "statues of God walking about in a Garden," endowed with a strength and beauty all our own. All that we ever wished we could be, we were— and more. We were fully alive.

So God created man in his own image, in the image of God he created him; male and female he created them. (Gen. 1:27)

When I look at the night sky and see the work of your fingers—
    the moon and the stars you have set in place—
what are mortals that you should think of us,
    mere humans that you should care for us?
For you made us only a little lower than God,
    and you crowned us with glory and honor. (Ps. 8:3–5 NLT)

I daresay we've heard a bit about original sin, but not nearly enough about original glory, which comes *before* sin and is deeper to our nature. We were crowned with glory and honor. Why does a woman long to be beautiful? Why does a man hope to be found brave? Because we remember, if only faintly, that we were once more than we are now. The reason you doubt there could be a glory to your life is because that glory has been the object of a long and brutal war.

For lurking in that Garden was an Enemy. This mighty angel had once been glorious as well, the captain of the Lord's hosts, beautiful and powerful beyond compare. But he rebelled against his Creator, led a great battle against the forces of heaven, and was cast down. Banished from his heavenly home, but not destroyed, he waited for an opportunity to take his revenge. Unable to over-throw the Mighty One, he turned his sights on those who bore his image. He lied to us about where true life was to be found, and we believed him. We fell, and "our glory faded," as Milton said, "faded so soon." Or as David lamented, "You turn my glory into shame" (Ps. 4:2).

But God did not abandon us, not by a long shot. I think even a quick read of the Old Testament would be enough to convince you that *war* is a central theme of God's activity. There is the Exodus, where God goes to war to set his captive people free. Blood. Hail.

Locusts. Darkness. Death. Plague after plague descends on Egypt like a boxer's one-two punch, like the blows of some great ax. Pharaoh releases his grip, but only for a moment. The fleeing slaves are pinned against the Red Sea when Egypt makes a last charge, hurtling down on them in chariots. God drowns those soldiers in the sea, every last one of them. Standing in shock and joy on the opposite shore, the Hebrews proclaim, "The LORD is a warrior!" (Ex. 15:3). Yahweh is a warrior.

Then it's war to get *to* the promised land. Moses and company have to do battle against the Amalekites; again God comes through, and Moses shouts, "The LORD will be at war against the Amalekites from generation to generation" (Ex. 17:16). Yahweh will be at war. Indeed. You ain't seen nothin' yet. Then it's war to get *into* the promised land—Joshua and the battle of Jericho, all that. After the Jews gain the promised land, it's war after war to *keep* it. Israel battles the Canaanites, the Philistines, the Midianites, the Egyptians again, the Babylonians—and on and on it goes. Deborah goes to war; Gideon goes to war; King David goes to war. Elijah wars against the prophets of Baal; Jehoshaphat battles the Edomites. Are you getting the picture?

Many people think the theme of war ends with the Old Testament. Not at all. Jesus says, "I did not come to bring peace, but a sword" (Matt. 10:34). In fact, his birth involved another battle in heaven:

> A great and wondrous sign appeared in heaven: a woman clothed with the sun, with the moon under her feet and a crown of twelve stars on her head. She was pregnant and cried out in pain as she was about to give birth. Then another sign appeared in heaven: an enormous red dragon with seven heads and ten horns and seven crowns on his heads . . . The dragon stood in front of the woman who was about to give birth, so that he might devour

her child the moment it was born. She gave birth to a son, a male child, who will rule all the nations with an iron scepter . . . And there was war in heaven. Michael and his angels fought against the dragon, and the dragon and his angels fought back. But he was not strong enough, and they lost their place in heaven . . . Then the dragon was enraged at the woman and went off to make war against the rest of her offspring—those who obey God's commandments and hold to the testimony of Jesus. (Rev. 12:1–5, 7–8, 17)

The birth of Christ was an act of war, an *invasion*. The Enemy knew it and tried to kill him as a babe (Matt. 2:13). No pale-faced altar boy, the whole life of Christ is marked by battle and confrontation. He kicks out demons with a stern command. He rebukes a fever, and it leaves Peter's mother-in-law. He rebukes a storm, and it subsides. He confronts the Pharisees time and again to set God's people free from legalism. In a loud voice he wakes Lazarus from the dead. He descends to hell, wrestles the keys of hell and death from Satan, and leads a train of captives free (Eph. 4:8–9; Rev. 1:18). And when he returns, I might point out, Jesus will come mounted on a steed of war, with his robe dipped in blood, armed for battle (Rev. 19:11–15).

War is not just one among many themes in the Bible. It is *the* backdrop for the whole Story, the context for everything else. God is at war. He is trampling out the vineyards where the grapes of wrath are stored. And what is he fighting for? Our freedom and restoration. The glory of God is man fully alive. In the meantime, Paul says, *arm yourselves,* and the first piece of equipment he urges us to don is the belt of truth (Eph. 6:10–18). We arm ourselves by getting a good, solid grip on our situation, by getting some clarity on the battle over our lives. God's intentions toward us are life. Those intentions are opposed. Forewarned is forearmed, as the saying goes.

In *Mere Christianity,* in the chapter he so rightly titled "The Invasion," C. S. Lewis tried to clarify our situation:

> One of the things that surprised me when I first read the New Testament seriously was that it talked so much about a Dark Power in the universe—a mighty evil spirit who was held to be the Power behind death and disease, and sin. The difference is that Christianity thinks this Dark Power was created by God, and was good when he was created, and went wrong. Christianity agrees . . . this universe is at war.

YOU MUST FIGHT FOR YOUR LIFE

Until we come to terms with *war* as the context of our days we will not understand life. We will misinterpret 90 percent of what is happening around us and to us. It will be very hard to believe that God's intentions toward us are life abundant; it will be even harder not to feel that somehow we are just blowing it. Worse, we will begin to accept some really awful things about God. That four-year-old girl being molested by her daddy—that is "God's *will*"? That ugly divorce that tore your family apart—God wanted that to happen too? And that plane crash that took the lives of so many—that was desired by God?

Most people get stuck at some point because God appears to have abandoned them. He is not coming through. Speaking about her life with a mixture of disappointment and cynicism, a young woman recently said to me, "God is rather silent right now." Yes, it's been awful. I don't discount that for a moment. She is unloved; she is unemployed; she is under a lot. But her attitude strikes me as deeply naive, on the level of someone caught in a cross fire who asks, rather shocked and with a sense of betrayal, "God, why won't you make them stop firing at me?" I'm sorry, but that's not where we are right now. It's not where we are in the Story. That day is coming, *later,* when the lion shall lie down with the lamb and we'll beat swords into plowshares. For now, it's bloody battle.

It sure explains a whole heckuva lot.

Before he promised us life, Jesus warned that a thief would try to steal, kill, and destroy it. How come we don't think that the thief then actually steals, kills, and destroys? You won't understand your life, you won't see clearly what has happened to you or how to live forward from here, unless you see it as *battle*. A war against your heart. And you are going to need your whole heart for what's coming next. I don't mean what's coming next in the story I'm telling. I mean what's coming next in the life you're living. There are a few things I know, and one thing I do know is this: we don't see things as clearly as we ought to. As we *need* to. We don't understand what's happening around us or to us or to those we love, and we are practically clueless when it comes to the weight of our own lives and the glory that's being . . . held back.

Some of you don't see it yet. That's all right. We have a whole book ahead of us. If it's true that there is a great and fierce battle unfolding all around us—and against us—why isn't the enemy more visible? And if there is a glory to my life, well, then, why don't I see *that*? Why do I struggle so much, and where is that life God offers?

We don't see clearly because we don't see with the eyes of our heart.

CHAPTER TWO

THE EYES OF THE HEART

I pray also that the eyes of your heart may be enlightened.
—THE APOSTLE PAUL (EPH. 1:18)

I am concerned with a certain way of looking at life, which was created in me by the fairy tales, but has since been ratified by the mere facts.

—G. K. CHESTERTON

Two men are seated across from each other in a dark room. Outside, a thunderstorm rages in the night, shaking the old house to its foundations. Flashes of lightning are dimmed by heavy curtains, which been drawn because it is a *secret* meeting. This is the first time these men have ever met, though they have been searching for each other most of their lives. Not a moment too soon, their destinies have crossed. One of them, a tall black man dressed all in black, carries the aura of a spiritual master. The younger man, trying his best to conceal the fact that he is frightened and uncertain, might become his disciple. It all depends on a decision.

MORPHEUS: I imagine that right now you're feeling a bit like Alice, tumbling down the rabbit hole?

NEO: You could say that.

MORPHEUS: I can see it in your eyes. You have the look of a man who accepts what he sees because he's expecting to wake up. Ironically, this is not far from the truth. Do you believe in fate, Neo?

NEO: No.

MORPHEUS: Why?

NEO: Because I don't like the idea that I'm not in control of my life.

MORPHEUS: I know exactly what you mean. Let me tell you why you're here. You're here because you know something. *What* you know you can't explain. You feel it. You've felt it your entire life. There's something wrong with the world. You don't know what it is. But it's there, like a splinter in your mind, driving you mad. It is this feeling that has brought you to me. Do you know what I'm talking about?

NEO: The Matrix?

MORPHEUS: Do you want to know what it is?

[*Hesitantly, Neo nods his assent.*]

MORPHEUS: The Matrix is everywhere. It is all around us. Even now in this very room. You can see it when you look out your window, or when you turn on your television. You can feel it when you go to work, when you go to church, when you pay your taxes. It is the world that has been pulled over your eyes to blind you from the truth.

NEO: What truth?

MORPHEUS: That you are a slave, Neo. Like everyone else you were born into bondage, into a prison that you cannot taste or smell or touch. A prison for your mind. Unfortunately, no one can be told what the Matrix is. You must see it for yourself.

[*In each of his open palms, held forth as an offering, the older man is holding two capsules, one red, the other blue. He is offering the younger man a chance at the truth.*]

MORPHEUS: This is your last chance. After this, there is no turning back. You take the blue pill—the story ends, you wake up in your bed and you believe . . . whatever you want to believe. You take the red pill—you stay in Wonderland and I show you how deep the rabbit hole goes.

Neo takes the red pill; Lucy steps through the wardrobe; Aladdin rubs the lamp; Elisha prays that the eyes of his servant would be opened; Peter, James, and John follow Jesus up to the Mount of Transfiguration. And all of them discover that there is far more going on here than meets the eye. The film *The Matrix* is a parable, a metaphor—and though a dark story, it is far closer to reality and to your life than you probably have been led to believe. (I am referring only to the first film in the trilogy.) And the question Morpheus asks of Neo is a question the Scriptures ask each of us: Do you *want* to see?

HOW CAN WE REALLY SEE?

There is another man, an old man, a spiritual master. Life for him has also been full of adventure and battle and trial by fire. He, too, knows something that we do not. And he, too, is trying to help us see. He writes,

> Therefore we do not lose heart. Though outwardly we are wasting away, yet inwardly we are being renewed day by day. For our light and momentary troubles are achieving for us an eternal glory that far outweighs them all. So we fix our eyes not on what is seen, but on what is unseen. For what is seen is temporary, but what is unseen is eternal. (2 Cor. 4:16–18)

The first line grabs me by the throat. "Therefore we do not lose heart." Somebody knows how not to lose heart? I'm all ears. For we *are* losing heart. All of us. Daily. It is the single most unifying quality shared by the human race on the planet at this time. We are losing—or we have already lost—heart. That glorious, resilient image of God in us is fading, fading, fading away. And this man claims to know a way out. Now, to appreciate the weight of his words, you need some idea of what his life has been like. He is neither wealthy nor famous; his life has not been sheltered, as the saying goes. But he has seen visions, had encounters, you might say, with something beyond the walls of this world. Ever since then, things have gotten difficult. In his own words, he has

> been in prison more frequently, been flogged more severely, and been exposed to death again and again. Five times I received . . . forty lashes minus one. Three times I was beaten with rods, once I was stoned, three times I was shipwrecked, I spent a night and a day in the open sea, I have been constantly on the move. I have been in danger from rivers, in danger from bandits, in danger from my own countrymen . . . I have known hunger and thirst and have often gone without food; I have been cold and naked. (2 Cor. 11:23–27)

Not to mention that little incident against wild beasts in Ephesus. You get the picture. His life has been hard. It has been war. His vita reads like something out of Amnesty International. Somebody has been trying to shut him up or shut him down. He knows something; he has a secret to tell. So, how, Paul—*how?* How do we not lose heart?

> So we fix our eyes not on what is seen, but on what is unseen.
> (2 Cor. 4:18)

What? I let out a sigh of disappointment. *Now that's helpful. "Look at what you cannot see."* That sounds like Eastern mysticism, that sort of wispy wisdom dripping in spirituality but completely inapplicable to our lives. Life is an illusion. Look at what you cannot see. *What can this mean?* Remembering that a little humility can take me a long way, I give it another go. This wise old seer is saying that there is a way of looking at life, and that those who discover it are able to live from the heart no matter what. How do we do this? By seeing with the eyes of the heart. "I pray . . . that the eyes of your heart may be enlightened" (Eph. 1:18).

SEEING WITH THE HEART

"A sower went out to sow some seed . . ."
"A man fell into the hands of robbers . . ."
"Suppose a woman has ten silver coins and loses one . . ."
"There were ten virgins with ten lamps . . ."

Think of it. You are the Son of the living God. You have come to earth to rescue the human race. It is your job to communicate truths without which your precious ones will be lost . . . forever. Would you do it like *this*? Really now. A treasure hidden in a field? A lump of dough? Ten virgins and something about oil? Why doesn't he come right out and say it—get to the point? What's with all the stories? Some of them rather puzzling, I might add. Jesus is not entertaining children; he is speaking to adults about the deepest things in life. And I think it's safe to say he knows quite well what he's doing. As Dallas Willard reminds us, Jesus is brilliant. He is the smartest man who ever lived. So what's up with all the stories?

We children of the Internet and the cell phone and the Weather Channel, we think we are the enlightened ones. We aren't fooled by anything—we just want the *facts*. The bottom line. So proposition has become our means of saying what is true and what is not. And proposition is helpful . . . for certain things. Sacramento is the capital of California; water freezes at 32 degrees Fahrenheit; your shoes are in the front room, under the sofa. But proposition fails when it comes to the weightier things in life. While it is a fact that the Civil War was fought between the years of 1861 and 1865 and while it is also a fact that hundreds of thousands of men died in that war, those facts hardly describe what happened at Bull Run or Antietam, at Cold Harbor or Gettysburg. You don't even begin to grasp the reality of the Civil War until you hear the stories, see pictures from the time, visit the battlefields, watch a film like *Glory*.

How much more so when it comes to the deep truths of the Christian faith. God loves you; you matter to him. That is a fact, stated as a proposition. I imagine most of you have heard it any number of times. Why, then, aren't we the happiest people on earth? It hasn't reached our hearts. Facts stay lodged in the mind, for the most part. They don't speak at the level we need to hear. Proposition speaks to the mind, but when you tell a story, you speak to the heart. We've been telling each other stories since the beginning of time. It is our way of communicating the timeless truths, passing them down.

And that's why when Jesus comes to town, he speaks in a way that will get past all our intellectual defenses and disarm our hearts. He tells a certain kind of story. As Chesterton said, "I am concerned with a certain way of looking at life, which was created in me by the fairy tales, but has since been ratified by the mere facts." And the best stories of all, the ones that bring us the Eternal Truths, they always take the form of parable or, sometimes we say, fairy tale. Better still to call them *myths*.

MYTHIC REALITY

And already I've lost many of you. For most of us rationalists, the word means "not true." Isn't that what you think when you hear someone say, "Oh, that's just a myth"? Meaning, that's not *factually* true. But myth is a story, like a parable, that speaks of Eternal Truths. I am not using *myth* in a technical way, referring to ancient Greek mythology. I am using it more broadly, more inclusively, to mean "a story that brings you a glimpse of the eternal" or "any story that awakens your heart to the deep truths of life." That is the unifying quality of all mythic stories, whether they be Sisyphus or *Sleeping Beauty* or *The Matrix*. Christian professor Rolland Hein has described it this way: "Myths are, first of all, stories: stories which confront us with something transcendent and eternal . . . a means by which the eternal expresses itself in time."

Jesus tells a story about a sower who went out to sow some seed. The year is uncertain; so is the identity of the sower in question. He and his seed are metaphors for something far more significant than a farmer and a bag of corn. In this case, they are symbols for the Son of God and the eternal Word. The story is meant for all of us, and so it transcends time and space and speaks for centuries. Myths are like that. They are stories that remind us of the transcendent and the eternal. Note the success of the *Star Wars* films or, more recently, *The Lord of the Rings* trilogy. Millions of people have enjoyed them—and more than once. It isn't because we think the stories are true in a factual sense. We don't even stop to ask the question about their historical accuracy or their scientific possibility. Their appeal lies deeper, in the realm of the heart.

Former Wheaton College professor of literature Clyde Kilby explains, "Myth is the name of a way of seeing, a way of *knowing*." Not fantasy, not lies, but things coming to us from beyond the walls of this world. Rolland Hein observes, "They are the kind of story that wakes you up, and suddenly you say, 'Yes, yes, this is what my life has really been about! Here is where my meaning and my destiny lie!'" And we need some waking up, you and I. We are, for the most part, alert and oriented times zero.

Years ago a mother wrote to C. S. Lewis regarding her son (age nine) and his love for *The Chronicles of Narnia*. The boy was feeling bad because he felt he loved Aslan (the lion hero of the story) more than Jesus. With grace and brilliance Lewis replied that he need not worry: "For the things he loves Aslan for doing or saying are simply the things that Jesus really did and said. So that when Laurence thinks he is loving Aslan, he is really loving Jesus: and perhaps loving Him more than he ever did before." Truth doesn't need a verse attached to it to be true. All that you loved about Aslan *is* Jesus.

"Systemizing flattens," says Kilby, "but myth rounds out. Systemizing drains away color and life, but myth restores. Myth is necessary because of what man is . . . because man is fundamentally mythic. His real health depends upon his knowing and living his . . . mythic nature." Mythic stories help us to see clearly, which is to say, they help us see with the eyes of the heart. So cast a wide net, and draw in all those stories that have ever stirred your soul, quickened your spirit, brought you to tears or joy or heroic imagination. You will need them all, as you shall see.

THINGS ARE NOT WHAT THEY SEEM

What do all the great stories and myths tell us? What do they have in common? What are they trying to get across? Wherever they may come from, whatever their shape might be, they nearly always speak to us Three Eternal Truths. First, these stories are trying to remind us that *things are not what they seem*. There is a whole lot more going on here than meets the eye. Much more. After the tornado sets her down, Dorothy wakes and steps out of her old farmhouse to find herself in a strange new world, a land of Munchkins and fairies and wicked witches. The Land of Oz. How brilliant for the filmmakers to have waited for this moment to introduce color in the movie. Up till now the story has been told in black and white; when Dorothy steps out of the house, the screen explodes in color, and she whispers to her little friend, "Toto . . . I don't think we're in Kansas anymore."

Alice falls through the rabbit hole into Wonderland. Adonos wakes to the sound of water and discovers a stream running right through his bedroom. The carpet that always looked to him like grass and flowers is, in fact, now just that—a meadow with daisies waving in a soft breeze. The ceiling above him has become the boughs of a great tree, "one of the advanced guard of a dense forest, towards which the rivulet ran. Faint traces of a footpath, much overgrown with grass and moss, were discernible along the right bank." He rightly assumes it must be the path into Fairy Land, and he rightly chooses to follow it.

Neo is awakened from the death-sleep of the Matrix to discover that the time is not 1999, but 2199, and the world he thought was real is actually a massive deception cast upon the human race to keep them prisoners. Jacob falls into a dream under the desert stars and sees a ladder "resting on the earth, with its top reaching to heaven, and the angels of God . . . ascending and descending on it" (Gen. 28:12). He wakes, more awake than he's ever been in his life, thanks to the dream, and realizes for the first time that there is more going on around him than he ever imagined. "Surely the LORD is in this place, and I was not aware of it" (28:16).

"And I was not aware of it." Isn't this the very lesson of the Emmaus Road? You recall the story—two followers of Christ are headed out of town after the Crucifixion, as dejected as two people can be, with every reason in their minds to be so and more. Their hopes have been shattered. They staked it all on the Nazarene, and now he's dead. As they slump back toward their homes, Jesus sort of sneaks up alongside, very much alive but incognito, and joins their conversation, feigning ignorance—and they not seeing it is him.

He asked them, "What are you discussing together as you walk along?"

They stood still, their faces downcast. One of them, named
Cleopas, asked him, "Are you only a visitor to Jerusalem and do
not know the things that have happened there in these days?"

"What things?" he asked.

"About Jesus of Nazareth," they replied. "He was a prophet,
powerful in word and deed before God and all the people. The
chief priests and our rulers handed him over to be sentenced to
death, and they crucified him; but we had hoped that he was the
one who was going to redeem Israel." (Luke 24:17–21)

"But we had hoped . . ." Ah, yes. We had hoped. I've a few
things in my life I could say that about. I imagine you could too. *I
had hoped . . .* The story is so human, so true to our lives. What is
so wonderful and hopeful and—because *we* know how it turns
out—also cracks me up is how they did not see. *They just didn't get
it.* They ignored the secret of the burning heart. For the story goes
on, as you may remember, and the mysterious Companion begins
to chide them for being "slow of heart to believe" as he reminds
them of the writings of the prophets, all the ancient wisdom. They
invite him to supper, and after another bit of feigning about need-
ing to move on, he does come in.

When he was at the table with them, he took bread, gave thanks,
broke it and began to give it to them. Then their eyes were
opened and they recognized him, and he disappeared from their
sight. They asked each other, "Were not our hearts burning
within us while he talked with us on the road and opened the
Scriptures to us?" (Luke 24:30–32)

Why do you suppose God gave us this story? Might it have been
to remind us that things are not what they seem? That our interpretation of events may be more than a little off? If we'll start there,
with a little humility, then we, too, might move on to have our eyes

opened to the rest of the story in *our* lives. There is more going on here than we imagined.

This is precisely what the Bible has warned us about all these years: that we live in two worlds—or better, in one world with two parts, one part that we can see and one part that we cannot. We are urged, for our own welfare, to act as though the unseen world (the rest of reality) is, in fact, more weighty and more real and more dangerous than the part of reality we can see. The lesson from the story of the Emmaus Road—the lesson the whole Bible is trying to get across—begins with this simple truth: things are not what they seem. There is more going on here than meets the eye. Far more. That is Eternal Truth Number One.

A Battle Is Under Way

But there is another, more urgent quality to every true myth. The Second Eternal Truth brought to us comes like a broken message over the radio or an urgent e-mail from a distant country, telling us that some great struggle or quest or battle is well under way. May even be hanging in the balance. When the four children stumble into Narnia, the country and all its lovely creatures are imprisoned under the spell of the White Witch and have been for a hundred years. In another story, Jack and his mother are starving and must sell their only cow. Frodo barely makes it out of the Shire with his life and the ring of power. In the nick of time he learns that Bilbo's magic ring is the One Ring, that Sauron has discovered its whereabouts, and that the Nine Black Riders are already across the borders searching for the little hobbit with deadly intent. The future of Middle Earth hangs on a thread.

Darth Vader just about has the universe under his evil fist when a pair of droids fall into the hands of Luke Skywalker. Luke has no idea what is unfolding, what great deeds have been done on his behalf, or what will be required of him in the battle to come. Sitting in a sandstone hut with old Ben Kenobi—he does not know this is the great Jedi warrior Obi-Wan Kenobi—Luke discovers the secret message from the princess: "This is our most desperate hour. Help me, Obi-Wan Kenobi. You're my only hope."

Again, this is *exactly* what the Scriptures have been trying to wake us up to for years. "Wake up, O sleeper . . . Be very careful, then, how you live . . . because the days are evil" (Eph. 5:14–16). Or as *The Message* has it: "So watch your step. Use your head. Make the most of every chance you get. These are desperate times!" Christianity isn't a religion about going to Sunday school, potluck suppers, being nice, holding car washes, sending our secondhand clothes off to Mexico— as good as those things might be. This is a world at war. Something large and immensely dangerous is unfolding all around us, we are caught up in it, and above all we doubt we have been given a key role to play. Do you think I'm being too dramatic? Consider the tale told in the book of Daniel, chapter 10.

In 605 B.C. the notorious Babylonians sacked Jerusalem. Among the hostages taken back to the city of the hanging gardens is a young man named Daniel. He becomes a sort of counselor among the royal cabinet, largely because God favors Daniel and reveals a number of mysteries to him that had stumped everyone else on staff. You might remember the famous episode when, in the midst of a state function turned Mardi Gras, King Belshazzar sees the handwriting on the wall—literally. *Mene, Mene, Tekel, Parsin.* Actually, everyone sees it, but only Daniel can interpret what it means. The Hebrew exile is right again, the king dies that night, the Medes take over, and after a number of additional years in the dangerous world of Middle Eastern politics, Daniel has another troubling vision. Let's pick up the story there.

In the third year of Cyrus king of Persia, a revelation was given to Daniel (who was called Belteshazzar). Its message was true and it concerned a great war. The understanding of the message came to him in a vision. At that time I, Daniel, mourned for three weeks. I ate no choice food; no meat or wine touched my lips; and I used no lotions at all until the three weeks were over. (Dan. 10:1–3)

Something has happened that Daniel doesn't understand. I think we can all relate to that. We don't understand about 90 percent of what happens to us, either. Daniel is troubled. He sets out to get an answer. But three weeks of prayer and fasting produce no results. What is he to conclude? If Daniel were like most people, by this point he'd probably be headed toward one of two conclusions: *I'm blowing it*, or *God is holding out on me*. He might try confessing every sin and petty offense in hopes of opening up the lines of communication with God. Or he might withdraw into a sort of disappointed resignation, drop the fast, and turn on the television. In an effort to hang on to his faith, he might embrace the difficulty as part of "God's will for his life." He might read a book on "the silence of God." That's the way the people I know handle this sort of thing.

And he would be dead wrong.

On the twenty-first day of the fast an angel shows up, out of breath. In a sort of apology, the angel explains to Daniel that God had actually dispatched him in answer to Daniel's prayers the very first day he prayed—three weeks ago. (There goes the whole unanswered prayer thesis, right out the window.) *Three weeks ago?* What is Daniel to do with that? "The very first day? But . . . I've . . . I mean, thank you so very much, and I don't want to seem ungrateful, but . . . where have you *been*?" You haven't blown it, Daniel, and God isn't holding out on you. The angel goes on to explain that he was locked in hand-to-hand combat with a mighty fallen angel, a demonic power of dreadful strength, who kept him out of the Persian kingdom for three weeks, and he finally had to get Michael (the great archangel, the captain of the Lord's hosts) to come and help him break through enemy lines. "Now I am here, in answer to your prayer. Sorry it's taken so long."

There it is—Eternal Truth Number Two: *this is a world at war.* We live in a far more dramatic, far more dangerous story than we ever imagined. The reason we love *The Chronicles of Narnia* or *Star Wars* or *The Matrix* or *The Lord of the Rings* is that they are telling us something about our lives that we never, ever get on the evening news. Or from most pulpits. *This is our most desperate hour.* Without this burning in our hearts, we lose the meaning of our days. It all withers down to fast food and bills and voice mail and who really cares anyway? Do you see what has happened? The essence of our faith has been stripped away. The very thing that was to give our lives meaning and *protect us*—this way of seeing—has been lost. Or stolen from us. Notice that those who have tried to wake us up to this reality were usually killed for it: the prophets, Jesus, Stephen, Paul, most of the disciples, in fact. Has it ever occurred to you that someone was trying to shut them up?

Things are not what they seem. This is a world at war. Now for the most stunning news of all.

THE WEIGHT OF YOUR GLORY

Last, but not least, not by a long shot, every mythic story *shouts* to us that in this desperate hour *we have a crucial role to play.* That is the Third Eternal Truth, and it happens to be the one we most desperately need if we are ever to understand our days. For most of his life, Neo sees himself only as Thomas Anderson, a computer programmer for a large software corporation. As the drama really begins to heat up and the enemy hunts him down, he says to himself, "This is insane. Why is this happening to me? What did I do? I'm nobody. I didn't do anything." A very dangerous conviction . . . though one shared by most of you, my readers. What he later comes to realize—and not a moment too soon—is that he is "the One" who will break the power of the Matrix.

Frodo, the little Halfling from the Shire, young and naive in so many ways, "the most unlikely person imaginable," is the Ring Bearer. He, too, must learn through dangerous paths and fierce battle that a task has been appointed to him, and if he does not find a way, no one will. Dorothy is just a farm girl from Kansas, who stumbled into Oz not because she was looking for adventure but because someone had hurt her feelings and she decided to run away from home. Yet she's the one to bring down the Wicked Witch of the West. Joan of Arc was also a farm girl, illiterate, the youngest in her family, when she received her first vision from God. Just about everyone doubted her; the commander of the French army said she should be taken home and given a good whipping. Yet she ends up leading the armies to war.

You see this throughout Scripture: a little boy will slay the giant, a loudmouthed fisherman who can't hold down a job will lead the church, and a whore with a golden heart is the one to perform the deed that Jesus asked us all to tell "wherever the gospel is preached throughout the world" (Mark 14:9). Things are not what they seem. *We* are not what we seem.

Of all the Eternal Truths we don't believe, this is the one we doubt most of all. Our days are not extraordinary. They are filled with the mundane, with hassles mostly. And we? We are . . . a dime a dozen. Nothing special really. Probably a disappointment to God. But as Lewis wrote, "The value of . . . myth is that it takes all the things we know and restores to them the rich significance which has been hidden by 'the veil of familiarity.'" You are not what you think you are. There is a glory to your life that your Enemy fears, and he is hell-bent on destroying that glory before you act on it. This part of the answer will sound unbelievable at first; perhaps it will sound too good to be true; certainly, you will wonder if it is true for you. But once you begin to see with those eyes, once you have begun to know it is true from the bottom of your heart, it will change everything.

The story of your life is the story of the long and brutal assault on your heart by the one who knows what you could be and fears it.

SEEING CLEARLY

> Do you think I am trying to weave a spell? Perhaps I am; but remember your fairy tales. Spells are used for breaking enchantments as well as for inducing them. And you and I have need of the strongest spell that can be found to wake us from the evil enchantment of worldliness which has been laid upon us for nearly a hundred years. (C. S. Lewis, *The Weight of Glory*)

Lewis is not being cute; he is as sober as a man can be. That evil enchantment of worldliness is the way of looking at life given to us by the Enlightenment, the Age of Reason, the modern era. Science as our interpreter. The Matrix. We all drank deeply from that cup—the church included—and now the whole kingdom lies under a spell, like Narnia in winter, like the sleeping kingdom in *Sleeping Beauty*. Or as the Bible has it, "The whole world lies under the power of the evil one" (1 John 5:19 NRSV). We've never stopped to think about it. How? *How* does the whole world lie under the power of the Evil One? They don't see. They are in a fog, under a spell. Their hearts are shrouded (2 Cor. 3:15; 4:3–6). O God, take this shroud away.

You will not think clearly about your life until you think mythically. Until you see with the eyes of your heart.

About halfway through their journey—following a great deal of hardship and facing a good deal more—Frodo's devoted friend and servant, Sam Gamgee, wonders out loud: "I wonder what sort of tale we've fallen into?" Sam is at that moment thinking mythically. He is wondering in the right way. His question assumes that there *is* a story; there is something larger going on. He also assumes that they have somehow tumbled into it, been swept up into it. This is exactly what we've lost. Things happen to you. The car breaks down, you have a fight with your spouse, or you suddenly figure out how to fix a problem at work. What is *really* happening? David Whyte says that we live our lives under a pale sky, "the lost sense that we play out our lives as part of a greater story."

What sort of tale have I fallen into? is a question that would help us all a great deal if we wondered it for ourselves. After my friend Julie saw *The Fellowship of the Ring,* she turned to the girl with her and whispered, "We've just gotten a clearer view of reality than we usually see." Yes—that's the kind of "seeing" we need; that *is* our reality. What grabbed me was the theatrical trailer for the film. In a brilliantly crafted three-minute summary, the preview captures the essential mythic elements of the story. As scene after scene races before the eyes of the viewer, and Gandalf describes the tale, these lines cross the screen:

Fate has chosen him.
A Fellowship will protect him.
Evil will hunt him.

Yes—that's it. That is the life Christianity is trying to explain to the world. Better, that is the reality into which Christianity is the door. If we could believe that about our lives, and come to *know* that it is true, everything would change. We would be so much more able to interpret the events unfolding around us, against us. We would discover the task that is ours alone to fulfill. We would find our courage. The hour is late, and you are needed. So much hangs in the balance. Where *is* your heart?

CHAPTER THREE

THE HEART OF ALL THINGS

Above all else, guard your heart,
　　for it is the wellspring of life.

　　　　　　　　　　　—KING SOLOMON (PROV. 4:23)

You are never a great man when you have more mind than heart.

　　　　　　　　　　　　　　　—BEAUCHENE

On her journey down the yellow brick road—a journey, may I remind you, that grows more dangerous every step she takes— Dorothy meets a number of strange sights. She befriends the Scarecrow, and later the two of them come upon a lumberjack made of tin, standing utterly still in the forest, his ax frozen in midair. At first, he seems unable to speak. Coming closer, they discover that he is trying to say something after all. *Oil . . . can.* After a bit more misunderstanding and misinterpretation, they get the oil can to the joints of his mouth, only to find that he can speak as well as any man, but that he was rusted. Once he is freed from his prison, he begins to tell them his story.

Now the movie left out a crucial point, which the author gave in his original fairy tale. The Tin Woodman had once been a *real* man, who had been in love with a beautiful maiden. It was his dream to marry her, once he could earn enough money to build them a cottage in the woods. The Wicked Witch hated his love, and she cast spells upon the man that caused him injury, so that one by one his limbs needed to be replaced with artificial ones, made of tin. At first it seemed an advantage, for his metal frame allowed him to work nearly as powerfully as a machine. With a heart of love and arms that never tired, he seemed sure to win.

"I thought I had beaten the Wicked Witch then, and I worked harder than ever; but I little knew how cruel my enemy could be. She thought of a new way to kill my love for the beautiful Munchkin maiden, and made my axe slip again, so that it cut right through my body, splitting it into two halves. Once more the tinner came to my help and made me a body of tin. Fastening my tin arms and legs and head to it, by means of joints, so that I could move around as well as ever. But alas! I now had no heart, so that I lost all my love for the Munchkin girl, and did not care whether I married her or not . . .

"My body shone so brightly in the sun that I felt very proud of it and it did not matter now if my axe slipped, for it could not cut me. There was only one danger—that my joints would rust; but I kept an oil-can in the cottage and took care to oil myself whenever I needed it. However, there came a day when I forgot to do this, and, being caught in a rainstorm, before I had thought of the danger my joints had rusted, and I was left to stand in the woods until you came to help me.

"It was a terrible thing to undergo, but during the year I stood there I had time to think that the greatest loss I had known was the loss of my heart. While I was in love I was the happiest man on earth; but no one can love who has not a heart, and so I am resolved to ask Oz to give me one. If he does, I will go back to the Munchkin maiden and marry her."

Both Dorothy and the Scarecrow had been greatly interested in the story of the Tin Woodman, and now they knew why he was so anxious to get a new heart. "All the same," said the Scarecrow, "I shall ask for brains instead of a heart; for a fool would not know what to do with a heart if he had one." "I shall take the heart," returned the Tin Woodman; "for brains do not make one happy, and happiness is the best thing in the world." (L. Frank Baum, *The Wonderful Wizard of Oz*)

Notice, there was a man who was once real and alive and in love. But after a series of blows, his humanity was reduced to efficiency. He became a sort of machine—a hollow man. At first, he did not even notice, for his condition made him an excellent woodman, as any person can become productive like a machine when he forgoes his heart. Notice also that it was the Wicked Witch who brought the disaster upon him. Baum's mythic tale reminds us that the Enemy knows how vital the heart is, even if we do not, and all his forces are fixed upon its destruction. For if he can disable or deaden your heart, then he has effectively foiled the plan of God, which was to create a world where love reigns. By taking out your heart, the Enemy takes out *you,* and you are essential to the Story.

You'll notice he's been rather effective.

I find it almost hard to believe a case must be made that the heart is . . . well, at the heart of it all. Of life. Of each person. Of God. And of Christianity. But our Enemy has come against us, and now we are all in some way like the Tin Woodman. We, too, have suffered a series of blows over time. And we, too, have seized upon efficiency, busyness, and productivity as the life we will live instead. Now we are lost. Dazed. Alert and oriented times zero.

Sleepwalking through life. In order to find our way out of these woods, we must return to the heart.

THE HEART IS CENTRAL

The heart is central. That we would even need to be reminded of this only shows how far we have fallen from the life we were meant to live—or how powerful the spell has been. The subject of the heart is addressed in the Bible more than any other topic—more than works or service, more than belief or obedience, more than money, and even more than worship. Maybe God knows something we've forgotten. But of course—all those other things are matters of the heart. Consider a few passages:

> Love the LORD your God with all your heart and with all your soul and with all your strength. (Deut. 6:5) [Jesus called this the greatest of all the commandments—and notice that the heart comes first.]

> Man looks at the outward appearance, but the LORD looks at the heart. (1 Sam. 16:7)

> Where your treasure is, there your heart will be also. (Luke 12:34)

> Trust in the LORD with all your heart,
> and lean not on your own understanding. (Prov. 3:5)

> Your word I have treasured in my heart,
> That I may not sin against You. (Ps. 119:11 NASB)

> These people honor me with their lips,
> but their hearts are far from me. (Matt. 15:8)

For the eyes of the LORD range throughout the earth to strengthen those whose hearts are fully committed to him. (2 Chron. 16:9)

All a man's ways seem right to him,
    but the LORD weighs the heart. (Prov. 21:2)

According to the Scriptures, the heart can be troubled, wounded, pierced, grieved, even broken. How well we all know that. Thankfully, it can also be cheerful, glad, merry, joyful, rejoicing. The heart can be whole or divided—as in that phrase we often use, "Well, part of me wants to, but the other part of me doesn't." It can be wise or foolish. It can be steadfast, true, upright, stout, valiant. (All of these descriptions can be found by perusing the listings for the word *heart* in any concordance.) It can also be frightened, faint, cowardly, melt like wax. The heart can be wandering, forgetful, dull, stubborn, proud, hardened. Wicked and perverse. I think we know that as well.

Much to our surprise, according to Jesus, a heart can also be pure, as in, "Blessed are the pure in heart, for they will see God" (Matt. 5:8). And even noble, as in his story about the sower: "But the seed on good soil stands for those with a noble and good heart, who hear the word, retain it, and by persevering produce a crop" (Luke 8:15). The Bible sees the heart as the source of all creativity, courage, and conviction. It is the source of our faith, our hope, and of course, our love. It is the "wellspring of life" within us (Prov. 4:23), the very essence of our existence, the center of our being, the fount of our life.

Think about your work life for a moment. Why are so many people bored or frustrated with their jobs? Why do they dread Monday morning and "thank God it's Friday"? Their hearts are not in their work. Far from it. However they arrived at what they're doing with their lives, it wasn't by listening to their heart. The same holds true for their love life. Why do so many relationships fail? Because one or both partners no longer have a heart for making it work. On and on it goes. Why are so many people struggling with depression and discouragement? They've lost heart. Why can't we seem able to break free of our addictions? Because somewhere along the way, in a moment of carelessness or desperation, we gave our heart away, and now we can't get it back.

There is no escaping the centrality of the heart. God knows that; it's why he made it the central theme of the Bible, just as he placed the physical heart in the center of the human body. The heart is central; to find our lives, we must make it central again.

REASON AND EMOTION

The mind receives and processes *information:*

- The boiling point of water is 212 degrees Fahrenheit.
- Lincoln was our sixteenth president.
- Light travels at a speed of 186,282 miles per second.

The heart knows and wrestles with *realities:*

- Your son is missing in combat.
- God has heard your prayers.
- Your daughter is getting married tomorrow.
- You are now and always have been loved.

The mind deals in *abstractions*:

- 2+2 = 4.
- You should get an oil change every three thousand miles.
- The phone company is increasing local service charges by $1.75.

The mind takes in and processes information. It is a beautiful gift of God. Why, you are using your mind even now on your search for

God and for life. But it remains, for the most part, indifferent. Your mind tells you that it is now 2:00 A.M. and your daughter has not returned, for the car is not in the driveway. Your heart wrestles with whether or not it is cause for worry.

The heart lives in the far more bloody and magnificent realities of living and dying and loving and hating. That's why those who live from their minds are detached from life. Things don't seem to touch them very much; they puzzle at the way others are so affected by life, and they conclude others are emotional and unstable. Meanwhile, those who live from the heart find those who live from the mind . . . unavailable. Yes, they are physically present. So is your computer. This is the sorrow of many marriages, and the number one disappointment of children who feel entirely missed or misunderstood by their parents.

Yes, the heart is the source of our emotions. But we have equated the heart *with* emotion, and put it away for a messy and even dangerous guide. No doubt, many people have made a wreck of their lives by following an emotion without stopping to consider whether it was a good idea to do so. Neither adultery nor murder is a rational act. But equating the heart *with* emotion is the same nonsense as saying that love is a feeling. Surely, we know that love is more than *feeling* loving; for if Christ had followed his emotions, he would not have gone to the cross for us. Like any man would have been, he was afraid; in fact, he knew that the sins of the world would be laid upon him, and so he had even greater cause for hesitation (Mark 14:32–35). But in the hour of his greatest trial, his love overcame his fear of what loving would cost him.

Emotions are the *voice* of the heart, to borrow Chip Dodd's phrase. Not the heart, but its voice. They express the deeper movements of the heart, as when we weep over the loss of someone we love, or when we cheer at the triumph of a son's team at the state championships. The mind stands detached, but it is with the heart that we experience and respond to life in all its fullness. Francis de Sales said, "Love is the life of our heart. According to it we desire, rejoice, hope and despair, fear, take heart, hate, avoid things, feel sad, grow angry, and exult." The heart expresses itself through emotion, but it expresses itself in many other ways as well.

MOTIVES

You'll notice that those who live from the mind shed few tears. I wonder if that isn't the real reason they choose to hide there. For when we're honest, we'll admit that there are our *stated* reasons for doing any of the things we do, and then there are our *real* reasons. We call them our motives.

Your wife asks why you turned to look at the pretty young thing in the tight jeans, and you defend yourself by saying that she only reminded you of Aunt Ruth. Yes, and people put radar detectors in their cars because they want to make sure they're maintaining the speed limit. Was it out of love that you remembered your anniversary, or was it fear that you'd be in serious trouble if you didn't? You flatter your boss. Does it have anything to do with the fact that your annual review is next week? What makes the Day of Judgment so unnerving is that all our posing and all our charades will be pulled back, all secrets will be made known, and our Lord will "expose the motives of men's *hearts*" (1 Cor. 4:5, emphasis added).

This is the point of the famous Sermon on the Mount. Jesus first says we haven't a hope of heaven unless our righteousness "surpasses that of the Pharisees" (Matt. 5:20). How can that be? They were fastidious rule keepers, pillars of the church, model citizens. Yes, Jesus says, and most of it was hypocrisy. The Pharisees prayed to impress men with their spirituality. They gave to impress men with their generosity. Their actions looked good, but their motives were not. Their hearts, as the saying goes, weren't in the right place.

A person's character is determined by his motives, and motive is always a matter of the heart. This is what Scripture means when it says that man looks at the outward appearance, but God looks at the heart. God doesn't judge us by our looks or our intelligence; he judges us by our hearts.

It makes sense, then, that Scripture also locates our conscience in our hearts. Paul says that even those who do not know God's law "show that the requirements of the law are written on their hearts, their consciences also bearing witness" (Rom. 2:15), such as when your child looks guilty for having told a lie. This is why it is so dangerous to harden our hearts by silencing our consciences, and why the offer of forgiveness is such good news, to have our "hearts sprinkled clean from an evil conscience" (Heb. 10:22 NRSV). Oh, the joy of living from right motives, from a clean heart. I doubt that those who want to dismiss the heart want to dismiss our consciences, set aside the importance of character.

THE THOUGHTS OF THE HEART

This is not to say the heart is only swirling emotion, mixed motives, and dark desire, without thought or reason. Far from it. According to Scripture, the heart is also where we do our deepest thinking. "Jesus, knowing what they were thinking in their hearts," is a common phrase in the Gospels. This might be most surprising to those who have accepted the Great Modern Mistake that "the mind equals reason and the heart equals emotion." Most people believe that. I heard it again, just last night, from a very astute and devoted young man. "The mind is our reason; the heart is emotion," he said. What popular nonsense. Solomon is remembered as the wisest man ever, and it was not because of the size of his brain. Rather, when God invited him to ask for anything in all the world, Solomon asked for a wise and discerning *heart* (1 Kings 3:9).

Our deepest thoughts are held in our hearts. Scripture itself claims to be "sharper than any double-edged sword, it penetrates even to dividing soul and spirit, joints and marrow; it judges the thoughts and attitudes of the heart" (Heb. 4:12). Not the feelings of the heart, the *thoughts* of the heart. Remember, when the shepherds reported the news that a company of angels had brought them out in the field, Mary "pondered them in her heart" (Luke 2:19), as you do when some news of great import keeps you up in the middle of the night. If you have a fear of heights, no amount of reasoning will get you to go bungee jumping. And if you are asked why you're paralyzed at the thought of it, you won't be able to explain. It is not rational, but it is your conviction nonetheless. Thus, the writer of Proverbs preempts Freud by about two thousand years when he states, "As [a man] thinketh in his heart, so is he" (Prov. 23:7 KJV). It is the thoughts and intents of the *heart* that shape a person's life.

The apostle Paul drives this home when he states: "If you confess with your mouth, 'Jesus is Lord,' and believe in your heart that God raised him from the dead, you will be saved. For it is with your heart that you believe and are justified" (Rom. 10:9–10). Read that again more slowly. "It is with your *heart* that you believe." Where does saving faith come from? The heart. Which raises a troubling reality for all of us: you do not belong to God, you are not a Christian at all, until you engage your heart, believe *with your heart*. Jesus said the same when, in a moment of frustration with his own people, he cried,

> For this people's heart has become calloused;
>> they hardly hear with their ears,
>> and they have closed their eyes.
> Otherwise they might see with their eyes,
>> hear with their ears,
>> *understand with their hearts*
> and turn, and I would heal them. (Matt. 13:15, emphasis added)

The mind is a faculty, and a magnificent one at that. But the heart is the dwelling place of our *true* beliefs.

MEMORY, CREATIVITY, AND COURAGE

Why is it, as Frederick Buechner said, that "a fragrance in the air, a certain passage of a song, an old photograph falling out from the pages of a book, the sound of somebody's voice in the hall . . . makes your heart leap and fills your eyes with tears"? Because the storehouse of your memory is held in your heart. We have a shard of this left in that expression we use: "I've learned it by heart," meaning, we have it inscribed into memory. But the faculty is far more than rote memorization; it is in the heart that we hang on to the most important things. In his last warning to the people of Israel, Moses urges them to "be careful, and watch yourselves closely so that you do not forget the things your eyes have seen *or let them slip from your heart* as long as you live" (Deut. 4:9, emphasis added). Memory is vital, and memory is a function of the heart.

Creativity flows from the heart as well. You can paint by the numbers, but the result will lack something essential to art. After God gave Moses detailed plans for the construction of the tabernacle—which was designed to be quite beautiful—he said, "'I have put wisdom in the hearts of all the gifted artisans, that they may make all that I have commanded you' . . . Then Moses called Bezalel and Aholiab, and every gifted artisan in whose heart the LORD had put wisdom, everyone whose heart was stirred, to come and do the work" (Ex. 31:6; 36:2 NKJV). Machines mass-produce units; but creative work flows from the heart of a person.

And then there is courage, "the first of human qualities," as Churchill knew, "because it is the quality which guarantees all the others." Indeed. It takes courage to love, doesn't it? It takes courage to trust someone with your life. It takes courage to believe what you cannot see. It takes courage to follow Christ. "Do not let your hearts be troubled and do not be afraid," he said (John 14:27). And with good reason. This life we are living takes great courage, more and more as we see what's really at stake here. "Hear, O Israel, today you are going into battle against your enemies. Do not be faint-hearted" (Deut. 20:3).

Working with a trowel in one hand and a sword in the other, the people of Israel rebuilt the wall of their fallen city: "We rebuilt the wall till all of it reached half its height, for the people worked with all their heart" (Neh. 4:6). So it is with any great project we under-take, especially this great endeavor of living. Success or failure can be pretty well predicted by the degree to which the heart is fully in it. Our word *courage* comes down to us from the Old French *cuer,* which came from the Latin *cor,* which means "heart." This battle for the heart is going to take all the courage you can muster. Heaven forbid you leave that heart behind.

THE POINT OF ALL LIVING

I love watching a herd of horses grazing in an open pasture or run-ning free across the sage-covered plateaus in Montana. I love hik-ing in the high country when the wildflowers are blooming—the purple lupine and the Shasta daisies, the Indian paintbrush when it's turning magenta. I love thunderclouds, massive ones. My fam-ily loves to sit outside on summer nights and watch the lightning, hear the thunder as a storm rolls in across Colorado. I love water too—the ocean, streams, lakes, rivers, waterfalls, rain. I love jump-ing off high rocks into lakes with my boys. I love old barns, wind-mills, the West. I love vineyards. I love it when Stasi is loving something, love watching her delight. I love my boys. I love God.

Everything you love is what makes a life worth living. Take a moment, set down the book, and make a list of all the things you love. Don't edit yourself; don't worry about prioritizing or anything of that sort. Simply think of all the things you love. Whether it's the people in your life or the things that bring you joy or the places that are dear to you or your God, you could not love them if you did not have a heart. A life filled with loving is a life most like the one that God lives, which is life as it was meant to be (Eph. 5:1–2). And loving requires a heart alive and awake and free.

Of all the things that are required of us in this life, which is the most important? What is the real point of our existence? Jesus was confronted with the question point-blank one day, and he boiled it all down to two things: loving God and loving others. Do this, he said, and you will find the purpose of your life. Everything else will fall into place. Somewhere down inside we know it's true; we know love is the point. We know if we could truly love, and be loved, and never lose love, we would finally be happy. Gerald May wrote, "We are created by love, to live in love, for the sake of love." And is it even possible to love *without* your heart?

The heart is the connecting point, the meeting place between any two persons. The kind of deep soul intimacy we crave with God and with others can be experienced only from the heart. We don't want to be someone's project; we want to be the desire of their heart. May lamented, "By worshiping efficiency, the human race has achieved the highest level of efficiency in history, but how much have we grown in love?"

We've done the same to our relationship with God. Christians have spent their whole lives mastering all sorts of principles, done their duty, carried on the programs of their church . . . and never known God intimately, heart to heart. There is that troubling passage Jesus gives us when he says that in the final account of our lives, some folks who did all sorts of Christian things will be genuinely surprised not to be invited into heaven. It reads, "Many will say to me on that day, 'Lord, Lord, did we not'" do all sorts of

Christian things, amazing things? And Christ will say, "I never knew you" (Matt. 7:22–23). The point is not the activity—the point is intimacy with God. Attend a class and take in information; then use that information to change the way you live. None of that will bring you into intimacy with God, just as taking a course on anatomy won't help you love your spouse. "You will find me," God says, "when you seek me with all your heart" (Jer. 29:13).

What more can be said, what greater case could be made than this: to find God, you must look with all your heart. To remain present to God, you must remain present to your heart. To hear his voice, you must listen with your heart. To love him, you must love with all your heart. You cannot be the person God meant you to be, and you cannot live the life he meant you to live, unless you live from the heart.

THE MISSION

This is absurd. I'm trying to tell you why you should breathe. "Remember now—oxygen is crucial to your body's needs. All of the other functions depend on it. You should get plenty of oxygen every day. Inhale, exhale. Inhale, exhale. Wonderful! Now remember to do this every moment of every day." All my defense here seems so far from the actual experience of having your heart back. Go fall in love then. Do something heroic; save someone's life. Spend a month in some breathtaking spot, doing nothing productive at all. Take up painting. Have yourself a good laugh—the kind that sends tears down your face and makes you grip your side for the ache of it. Listen to a beautiful piece of music. Live with courage. Tuck your child into bed; listen to her prayers; kiss her cheek. Find God.

Then you will remember again that the heart is central. Not the mind, not the will. The heart.

So what, then, *is* the heart? "Heart in Scripture," notes Charles

Ryrie, "is considered the very center and core of life." That's right. The heart is the deep center of our life. "The innermost part of the human personality," says James Houston, "the center of those qualities that make us human." Yes, that's it. The heart is who we are. The real self. I think I like Oswald Chambers's definition most: "The use of the Bible term *heart* is best understood by simply saying 'me.'" Me. It puts us back together from all the psychological, scientific, and even theological dissection we've been handed by the Modern Era and gives us back a whole self. Me. My heart is me. The real me. Your heart is you. The deepest, truest you. That is why the heart is central, for what shall we do if we dismiss our self?

Christ did not die for an idea. He died for a person, and that person is you. But there again, we have been led astray. Ask any number of people why Christ came, and you'll receive any number of answers, but rarely the real one. "He came to bring world peace." "He came to teach us the way of love." "He came to die so that we might go to heaven." "He came to bring economic justice." On and on it goes, much of it based in a partial truth. But wouldn't it be better to let him speak for himself?

Jesus steps into the scene. He reaches back to a four-hundred-year-old prophecy to tell us why he's come. He quotes from Isaiah 61:1, which goes like this:

> The Spirit of the Sovereign LORD is on me,
>> because the LORD has anointed me
>> to preach good news to the poor.
> He has sent me to bind up the brokenhearted,
>> to proclaim freedom for the captives
>> and release from darkness for the prisoners.

The meaning of this quotation has been clouded by years of religious language and ceremonial draping. What is he saying? It has something to do with good news, with healing hearts, with setting someone free. That much is clear from the text. Permit me a translation in plain language:

> God has sent me on a mission.
> I have some great news for you.
> God has sent me to restore and release something.
> And that something is you.
> I am here to give you back your heart and set you free.

Now, Christ could have chosen any one of a thousand other passages to explain his life purpose. He is the Sacrificial Lamb, the Root of Jesse, the Morning Star. But here, at the opening moment of his ministry, he chose this passage above all others; this is the heart of his mission. Everything else he says and does finds its place under this banner. I am here to give you back your heart and set you free. *That* is why the glory of God is man fully alive: it's what he said he came to do. But of course. The opposite can't be true. "The glory of God is man barely making it, a person hardly alive." How can it bring God glory for his very image, his own children, to remain so badly marred, broken, captive? Alert and oriented times zero?

How we've overlooked this is one of the great mysteries of our times. It is simply diabolical, despicable, downright *evil* that the heart should be so misunderstood, maligned, feared, and dismissed. But there is our clue again. The war we are in would explain so great a loss. This is the *last* thing the Enemy wants you to know. His plan from the beginning was to assault the heart, just as the Wicked Witch did to the Tin Woodman. Make them so busy, they ignore the heart. Wound them so deeply, they don't want a heart. Twist their theology, so they despise the heart. Take away their courage. Destroy their creativity. Make intimacy with God impossible for them.

Of course your heart would be the object of a great and fierce battle. It is your most precious possession. Without your heart you cannot have God. Without your heart you cannot have love. Without your heart you cannot have faith. Without your heart you cannot find the work that you were meant to do. In other words, without your heart you cannot have *life*. The question is, Did Jesus keep his promise? What has he done for our hearts?

The answer will astound you.

PART TWO

THE RANSOMED HEART

"The time is coming," declares the LORD,
   "when I will make a new covenant
with the house of Israel
   and with the house of Judah.
It will not be like the covenant
   I made with their forefathers
when I took them by the hand
   to lead them out of Egypt,
because they broke my covenant,
   though I was a husband to them," declares the LORD.
"This is the covenant I will make with the house of Israel
   after that time," declares the LORD.
"I will put my law in their minds
   and write it on their hearts.
I will be their God,
   and they will be my people."

—JEREMIAH 31:31–33

I will give you a new heart and put a new spirit in you; I will
remove from you your heart of stone and give you a heart of

flesh. And I will put my Spirit in you and move you to follow my decrees and be careful to keep my laws.

—Ezekiel 36:26–27

This we now know: the heart is central. It matters—deeply. When we see with the eyes of the heart, which is to say, when we see mythically, we begin to awaken, and what we discover is that things are not what they seem. We *are* at war. We must fight for the life God intends for us, which is to say, we must fight for our heart, for it is the wellspring of that life within us.

Standing in the way of the path to life—the way of the heart—is a monstrous barrier. It has stopped far too many pilgrims dead in their tracks, for far too long. There is a widespread belief among Christians today that the heart is desperately wicked—even after a person comes to Christ.

It is a crippling belief.

And it is untrue.

CHAPTER FOUR

RANSOMED AND RESTORED

Create in me a clean heart, O God.

—KING DAVID (PS. 51:10 NKJV)

I will give you a new heart.

—GOD (EZEK. 36:26)

Now Beauty feared that she had caused his death. She ran throughout the palace, sobbing loudly. After searching everywhere, she recalled her dream and ran into the garden toward the canal, where she had seen him in her sleep. There she found the poor Beast stretched out unconscious. She thought he was dead. Without concern for his horrifying looks, she threw herself on his body and felt his heart beating. So she fetched some water from the canal and threw it on his face.

Beast opened his eyes and said, "You forgot your promise, Beauty. The grief I felt upon having lost you made me decide to fast to death. But I shall die content since I have the pleasure of seeing you one more time."

"No, my dear Beast, you shall not die," said Beauty. "You will live to become my husband. I give you my hand, and I swear that I belong only to you from this moment on. Alas! I thought that I only felt friendship for you, but the torment I am feeling makes me realize that I cannot live without you."

Beauty had scarcely uttered these words when the castle radiated with light. Fireworks and music announced a feast. These attractions did not hold her attention, though. She returned her gaze to her dear Beast, whose dangerous condition made her tremble. How great was her surprise when she discovered that the Beast had disappeared, and at her feet was a prince more handsome than Eros himself, who thanked her for putting an end to his enchantment.

It is the deepest and most wonderful of all mythic truths, unveiled here in the original *Beauty and the Beast,* written by Jeanne-Marie Leprince de Beaumont. The Transformation. A creature that no one could bear to look upon is transformed into a handsome prince. That which was dark and ugly is now glorious and good. Is it not the most beautiful outcome of any story to be written? Perhaps that is because it is the deepest yearning of the human heart. Look how often this theme surfaces.

The phoenix rises from the ashes. Cinderella rises from the cinders to become a queen. The ugly duckling becomes a beautiful swan. Pinocchio becomes a real boy. The frog becomes a prince. Wretched old Scrooge becomes "as good a friend, as good a master, and as good a man as the good old city knew, or any other good old city, town or borough in the good old world." The Cowardly Lion gets his courage and the Scarecrow gets his brains and the Tin Woodman gets a new heart. In hope beyond hope, they are all transformed into the very thing they never thought they could be.

Why are we enchanted by tales of transformation? I can't think of a movie or novel or fairy tale that doesn't somehow turn on this. Why is it an essential part of any great story? Because it is the secret to Christianity, and Christianity is the secret to the universe. "You must be born again" (John 3:7). You must be transformed. Keeping the Law, following the rules, polishing up your manners—none of that will do. What counts is whether we really have been changed into new and different people (Gal. 6:15). Is this not the message of the gospel? Zacchaeus the trickster becomes Zacchaeus the Honest One. Mary the whore becomes Mary the Last of the Truly Faithful. Paul the self-righteous murderer becomes Paul the Humble Apostle.

And we? I doubt that many of us would go so far as to say we're *transformed*. Our names are written down somewhere in heaven, and we have been forgiven. Perhaps we have changed a bit in what we believe and how we act. We confess the creeds now, and we've gotten our temper under control . . . for the most part. But *transformed* seems a bit too much to claim. How about *forgiven and on our way?* That's how most Christians would describe what's happened to them. It's partly true . . . and partly *untrue,* and the part that's untrue is what's killing us. We've been told that even though we have placed our hope in Christ, even though we have become his followers, our *hearts* are still desperately wicked.

But is that what the Bible teaches?

WHAT WE MOST DESPERATELY NEED

"Everything I learned about human nature I learned from me," wrote the playwright Anton Chekhov, and the characters he so vividly created—with all their selfishness, their hatred, their dark and desperate desires, their hopelessness—they do rather well to describe us all. Imagine a story whose characters are taken from *your* own inner life and blown up for all to see. Egads. Something has gone wrong with the human race, and we know it. Better said, something has gone wrong *within* the human race. It doesn't take a theologian or a psychologist to tell you that. Read a newspaper. Spend a weekend with your relatives. Simply pay attention to the movements of your own heart in a single day. Most of the misery we suffer on this planet is the fruit of the human heart gone bad.

Scripture could not be more clear on this. Yes, God created us to reflect his glory, but barely three chapters into the drama we torpedoed the whole project. Sin entered the picture and spread like a computer virus. By the sixth chapter of Genesis, our downward spiral had reached the point where God himself couldn't bear it any longer: "The LORD saw how great man's wickedness on the earth had become, and that every inclination of the thoughts of his heart was only evil all the time. The LORD was grieved that he had made man on the earth, and his heart was filled with pain" (Gen. 6:5–6). This is the first mention of God's heart in the Bible, by the way, and it's a sad beginning, to be sure. His heart is broken because ours is fallen.

Any honest person knows this. We know we are not what we were meant to be. If we'll stop shifting the blame for just a moment, stop trying to put the onus on some other person or some policy or some other race, if we will take a naked and frank assessment of ourselves as measured against the life of Christ, well, then. Most of us will squirm and dodge and admit that perhaps we fall a bit short. If we're truly honest, we'll confess that we have it in us to be the Beast, the wicked stepsister, Scrooge. Most of the world religions concur on this point. Something needs to be done.

But the usual remedies involve some sort of shaping up on our part, some sort of face-lift whereby we clean up our act and start behaving as we should. Jews try to keep the Law. Buddhists follow the Eightfold Path. Muslims live by the Five Pillars. Many Christians try church attendance and moral living. You'd think, with all the effort, humanity would be on top of things by now. Of course, the reason all those treatments ultimately fail is that we quite misdiagnosed the disease. The problem is not in our behavior; the problem is *in us*. Jesus said, "For *out of the heart* come evil thoughts, murder, adultery, sexual immorality, theft, false testimony, slander" (Matt. 15:19, emphasis added). We don't need an upgrade. We need transformation. We need a miracle.

THE LAST ADAM, THE SECOND MAN

Jesus of Nazareth is given many names in Scripture. He is called the Lion of Judah. The Bright and Morning Star. The Wonderful Counselor. The Prince of Peace. The Lamb of God. There are many, many more—each one a window into all that he truly is, all that he has done, all that he will do. But one name seems to have escaped our attention, and that might help explain our misunderstanding of the gospel. Paul refers to Jesus as the Last Adam and the Second Man (1 Cor. 15:45–47). Why is this important? Because of what happened through the *First* Adam.

Our first father, Adam, and our first mother, Eve, were destined to be the root and trunk of humanity. What they were meant to be, we were meant to be: the kings and queens of the earth, the rulers over all creation, the glorious image bearers of a glorious God. They were statues of God walking about in a Garden, radiant Man and Woman, as we were to be. Our natures and our destinies were bound up in theirs. Their choices would forever shape our lives, for good or for evil. It is deep mystery, but we see something of a hint of it in the way children so often follow in the steps of their parents. Haven't you heard it said, "He has his father's temper," or "She has her mother's wit"? As the old saying goes, the fruit doesn't fall far from the tree. In fact, we call them family trees, and Adam and Eve are the first names on the list.

Our first parents chose, and it was on the side of evil. They broke the one command, the only command, God gave to them, and what followed you can watch any night on the news. The long lament of human history. Something went wrong in their hearts, something *shifted,* and that shift was passed along to each of us. Parents will often wonder where their toddlers learned to lie or how they came into the world so self-centered. It doesn't need to be taught to them; it is inherent to human nature. Paul makes clear in Romans, "Sin entered the world through one man . . . through the disobedience of the one man the many were made sinners" (5:12, 19). Of course, I am simply restating the doctrine of original sin, a core tenet of Christianity essential to Scripture.

But that is not the end of the Story, thank God. The First Adam was only "a pattern of the one to come" (Rom. 5:14). He would foreshadow another man, the head of a new race, the firstborn of a new creation, whose life would mean transformation to those who would become joined to him: "For just as through the disobedience of the one man [Adam] the many were made sinners, so also through the obedience of the one man [Christ, the Last Adam] the many will be made righteous" (Rom. 5:19).

A man comes down from heaven, slips into our world unnoticed, as Neo does in *The Matrix,* as Maximus does in *Gladiator,* as Wallace does in *Braveheart.* Yet he is no ordinary man, and his mission no ordinary mission. He comes as a substitute, a representative, as the destroyer of one system and the seed of something new. His death and resurrection break the power of the Matrix, release the prisoners, set the captives free. It is a historic fact. It really happened. And it is more than history. It is mythic in the first degree. Lewis said, "By becoming fact, it does not cease to be myth; that is the miracle."

In the fifth chapter of the famous book of Romans, Paul asks, Was Adam effective? Did his life have far-reaching consequences? We all know it did. It was devastating. He goes on to say, Well, then, the consequences of Christ, the Last Adam, were even greater:

"For if, by the trespass of the one man, death reigned through that one man, *how much more* will those who receive God's abundant provision of grace and of the gift of righteousness reign in life through the one man, Jesus Christ" (Rom. 5:17, emphasis added).

I WILL REMOVE YOUR HEART OF STONE

Jesus of Nazareth was sentenced to death by a vain puppet of the Roman government acting as district governor of Jerusalem. He was nailed to a cross by a handful of Roman soldiers who happened to be on duty, and left there to die. He died sometime around three o'clock in the afternoon on a Friday. Of a broken heart, by the way. And we call it Good Friday, of all strange things, because of what it effected. An innocent man, the Son of God, bleeding for the sins of the world. Standing in for us, as Jack gives his life for Rose in *Titanic,* as Sydney Carton stands in to die for Charles Darnay in *A Tale of Two Cities,* or as Aslan dies on the stone table to ransom the traitor Edmund. We rebelled, and the penalty for our rebellion was death. To lose us was too great a pain for God to bear, and so he took it upon himself to rescue us. The Son of God came "to give his life as a ransom for many" (Matt. 20:28).

You have been ransomed by Christ. Your treachery is forgiven. You are entirely pardoned for every wrong thought and desire and deed. This is what the vast majority of Christians understand as the central work of Christ for us. And make no mistake about it—it is a deep and stunning truth, one that will set you free and bring you joy. For a while.

But the joy for most of us has proven fleeting because we find that we need to be forgiven again and again and again. Christ has died for us, but we remain (so we believe) deeply marred. It actually ends up producing a great deal of guilt. "After all that Christ has done for you . . . and now you're back here asking forgiveness *again*?" To be destined to a life of repeating the very things that sent our Savior to the cross can hardly be called *salvation*.

Think of it: you are a shadow of the person you were meant to be. You have nothing close to the life you were meant to have. And you have no real chance of becoming that person or finding that life. However, you are forgiven. For the rest of your days, you will fail in your attempts to become what God wants you to be. You should seek forgiveness and try again. Eventually, shame and disappointment will cloud your understanding of yourself and your God. When this ongoing hell on earth is over, you will die, and you will be taken before your God for a full account of how you didn't measure up. But you will be forgiven. After that, you'll be asked to take your place in the choir of heaven. This is what we mean by *salvation*.

The good news is . . . that is *not* Christianity. There is more. *A lot more*. And that more is what most of us have been longing for most of our lives.

Under the old covenant, a Jewish boy was to be circumcised when he was eight days old, the foreskin of his penis removed with a knife. It was intended to be symbolic, a sign of the covenant given to Abraham. Forever after, everyone, including that boy, would know that he was marked for God, set apart for God. But in that symbol lay a deeper meaning, veiled for centuries, just as the mythic is often veiled, just as the sacrificial lamb required of the ancient Jews would foreshadow the death of Christ. It would take a Jewish convert of Christ to explain the true meaning of circumcision:

> A man is not a Jew if he is only one outwardly, nor is circumcision merely outward and physical. No, a man is a Jew if he is one inwardly; and circumcision is circumcision *of the heart*, by the Spirit, not by the written code. (Rom. 2:28–29, emphasis added)

In [Christ] you were also circumcised, in the putting off of the
sinful nature, not with a circumcision done by the hands of men
but with the circumcision done by Christ. (Col. 2:11)

It's not just that the Cross did something *for* us. Something deep
and profound happened *to* us in the death of Christ. Remember—the
heart is the problem. God understands this better than anyone, and
he goes for the root. God promised in the new covenant to "take away
your heart of stone." How? By joining us to the death of Christ. Our
nature was nailed to the cross with Christ; we died there, with him, in
him. Yes, it is a deep mystery—"deep magic" as Lewis called it—but
that does not make it untrue. "The death he died, he died to sin once
for all . . . In the same way, count yourselves dead to sin" (Rom.
6:10–11). Jesus was the Last Adam, the end of that terrible story.

You've been far more than forgiven. God has removed your heart
of stone. You've been delivered of what held you back from what
you were meant to be. You've been rescued from the part of you
that sabotages even your best intentions. Your heart has been circumcised to God. Your heart has been set free.

And there is even more.

AND I WILL GIVE YOU A NEW HEART

Most people assume that the Cross *is* the total work of Christ. The
two go hand in hand in our minds—Jesus Christ and the Cross; the
Cross and Jesus Christ. The Resurrection is impressive, but kind of
. . . an afterthought. It was needed, of course, to get him out of the
grave. Or the Resurrection is important because it proves Jesus was
the Son of God. His death was the *real* work on our behalf. The
Resurrection is like an epilogue to the real story; the extra point
after the touchdown; the medal ceremony after the Olympic event.
You can see which we think is more important. What image do we

put on our churches, our Bibles, our jewelry? The cross is the symbol of Christianity worldwide. However . . .

The cross was never meant to be the only or even the central symbol of Christianity.

That you are shocked by what I've just said only proves how far we've strayed from the faith of the New Testament. The cross is not the sole focal point of Christianity. Paul says so himself: "If Christ has not been raised, our preaching is useless and so is your faith . . . If Christ has not been raised, your faith is futile; you are still in your sins" (1 Cor. 15:14, 17).

> We have grown so used to the idea that the Crucifixion is the supreme symbol of Christianity, that it is a shock to realize how late in the history of Christian art its power was recognized. In the first art of Christianity it hardly appears; and the earliest example, on the doors of Santa Sabina in Rome [around A.D. 430], is stuck away in a corner, almost out of sight . . . early Christian art is concerned with miracles, healings, and with hopeful aspects of the faith like the Ascension and the Resurrection.

Art historian Kenneth Clark is telling us something so foreign to our thinking, it takes a second reading. What? Christians don't even begin to use the cross as a symbol until *four hundred years after Christ,* and then only in a minor role? *Four hundred years* of the earliest and most vibrant Christianity goes by without the cross as its rallying point?! Those who walked with Jesus, and those who walked with those who walked with Jesus—they didn't make the cross central? Why? As the record goes, what the apostles preached was the *Resurrection:*

> In those days Peter stood up among the believers (a group numbering about a hundred and twenty) and said, "Brothers, the

Scripture had to be fulfilled which the Holy Spirit spoke long ago through the mouth of David concerning Judas, who served as guide for those who arrested Jesus . . . Therefore it is necessary to choose one of the men who have been with us the whole time the Lord Jesus went in and out among us . . . For one of these must become a witness with us of his resurrection." (Acts 1:15–16, 21–22)

The priests and the captain of the temple guard and the Sadducees came up to Peter and John while they were speaking to the people. They were greatly disturbed because the apostles were teaching the people and proclaiming in Jesus the resurrection of the dead. (Acts 4:1–2)

With great power the apostles continued to testify to the resurrection of the Lord Jesus, and much grace was upon them all. (Acts 4:33)

Paul was preaching the good news about Jesus and the resurrection. (Acts 17:18)

The early Christian church symbolized the Resurrection, healings, and miracles because the church thought those things were central. The reason the first and closest friends of Jesus focused on miracles, healings, and hopeful aspects of the faith such as the Ascension and the Resurrection was simply that those are what God himself wants us to focus on. *Those are the point.* Those make Christianity such very good news. A dead man is not a great deal of help to us; a dead God is even worse. But life, real life, the power of God to *restore* you . . . now that's a whole nother matter.

We say Christ died for us, and that is true. But Christ was also *raised* for us. His resurrection was as much for us as his death was.

> For if, by the trespass of the one man [the First Adam], death reigned through that one man, how much more will those who receive God's abundant provision of grace and of the gift of righteousness *reign in life* through the one man, Jesus Christ. (Rom. 5:17, emphasis added)

> We were therefore buried with him through baptism into death in order that, just as Christ was raised from the dead through the glory of the Father, we too may live a new life . . . In the same way, count yourselves dead to sin but alive to God in Christ Jesus. (Rom. 6:4, 11)

> But because of his great love for us, God . . . made us alive with Christ. (Eph. 2:4–5)

Remember now—Adam was *a pattern* of the One to come. He was the root and trunk of our family tree. Our hearts fell when he fell. We received our sinful nature from him. So we now receive a *new* nature and a *new* heart from Christ, our Second Man. We have been made alive with the life of Christ. Just as we received our sinful nature from Adam, so we now receive a good and holy nature from Christ. It has always been God's plan not just to forgive you, but to restore you: "Make a tree good and its fruit will be good" (Matt. 12:33). Or as Milton had it,

> Their nature also to thy nature join . . .
> And live in thee transplanted, and from thee
> Receive new life.

Let me try this again. The new covenant has two parts to it: "I will give you a new heart and put a new spirit in you; I will remove from you your heart of stone and give you a heart of flesh" (Ezek.

36:26). God removed your old heart when he circumcised your heart; he gives you a new heart when he joins you to the life of Christ. That's why Paul can say "count yourselves dead to sin" *and* "alive to God in Christ Jesus" (Rom. 6:11).

> The story of the Incarnation is the story of a descent and resurrection . . . one has the picture of a diver, stripping off garment after garment, making himself naked, then flashing for a moment in the air, and then down through the green, and warm, and sunlit water into the pitch black, cold, freezing water, down into the mud and slime, then up again, his lungs almost bursting, back again to the green and warm and sunlit water, and then at last out into the sunshine, holding in his hand the dripping thing he went down to get. This thing is human nature. (C. S. Lewis, "The Grand Miracle")

The Resurrection affirms the promise Christ made. For it was *life* he offered to give us: "I have come that they may have life, and have it to the full" (John 10:10). We are saved by his life when we find that *we are able to live* the way we've always known we should live. We are free to be what he meant when he meant us. You have a new life—the life of Christ. And you have a new heart. Do you know what this means? Your heart is good.

THE DWELLING PLACE OF GOD

The year is about 1450 B.C. Somewhere in the deserts east of Sinai, a band of runaway slaves have pitched camp. In the middle of the camp, the nomads have erected a tent of goat hair and skins—a design given to them by God himself when he talked face-to-face with Moses on the mountain. The tabernacle had two parts, the Holy Place and the Most Holy Place (the Holy of

Holies). It was in the Most Holy Place that the presence of God would come: "Moses did everything just as the LORD commanded him . . . and the glory of the LORD filled the tabernacle" (Ex. 40:16, 34).

And just as Adam was a pattern of the One who was to come, just as the sacrificial lambs offered by the Jews in that tabernacle foreshadowed an even greater Sacrifice to come, so the tabernacle itself was a picture of something even more amazing. It is a kind of mythic symbol, given to us to help us understand a deeper eternal reality. Each person knows that now his *body* is the temple of God: "Do you not know that your body is a temple of the Holy Spirit, who is in you, whom you have received from God?" (1 Cor. 6:19). Indeed it is. "Don't you know that you yourselves are God's temple and that God's Spirit lives in you?" (1 Cor. 3:16). Okay—each of us is now the temple of God. So where, then, is the Holy of Holies?

Your heart.

That's right—your heart. Paul teaches us in Ephesians that "Christ may dwell in your hearts through faith" (3:17). God comes down to dwell in us, *in our hearts*. Now, we know this: God cannot dwell where there is evil. "You are not a God who takes pleasure in evil; with you the wicked cannot dwell" (Ps. 5:4). Something pretty dramatic must have happened in our hearts, then, to make them fit to be the dwelling place of a holy God.

Of course, none of this can happen for us until we give our lives back to God. We cannot know the joy or the life or the freedom of heart I've described here until we surrender our lives to Jesus and surrender them totally. Renouncing all the ways we have turned from God in our hearts, we forsake the idols we have worshiped and given our hearts over to. We turn, and give ourselves body, soul, and spirit back to God, asking him to cleanse our hearts and make them new. And he does. He gives us a new heart. And he comes to dwell there, in our hearts.

The Promise Fulfilled

"If we believed that . . . we could do *anything*. We would follow him *anywhere!*"

A few of us were sitting around last week talking about the gospel, what it really promises and what it means for our lives. I was trying to make the case that the new covenant means nothing less than this: the heart is good. I was surprised to hear the protests from most of my friends, who are deeply committed followers of Jesus and who have walked with him for years. "What? That can't be! I've never heard that . . . ever." I know. Neither had I. But it's undeniable: the new covenant, accomplished through the work of Christ, means that we have a new heart. Now listen to Jesus:

> Each tree is recognized by its own fruit. People do not pick figs from thornbushes, or grapes from briers. *The good man brings good things out of the good stored up in his heart,* and the evil man brings evil things out of the evil stored up in his heart. (Luke 6:44–45, emphasis added)

Later, explaining the parable of the sower and the seed, Jesus says,

> The seed on good soil stands for those *with a noble and good heart,* who hear the word, retain it, and by persevering produce a crop. (Luke 8:15, emphasis added)

Jesus himself teaches that at least for somebody, the heart can be good and even noble. That somebody is you, if you are his. God kept his promise. Our hearts have been circumcised to God. We have new hearts. Do you know what this means? Your heart is good. Let that sink in for a moment. Your heart is *good*.

What would happen if you believed it, if you came to the place where you *knew* it was true? Your life would never be the same. My friend Lynn got it, and that's when she exclaimed, "If we believed that . . . we could do *anything*. We would follow him *anywhere!*" Exactly. It would change our lives. It would change the face of Christianity. This is the lost message of the gospel, lost at least to a great many people. Small wonder. This is the *last* thing the Enemy wants the world to know. It would change everything. Those of you who've gotten your hearts back know exactly what I mean. It's freedom. It's life.

CHAPTER FIVE

THE GLORY HIDDEN IN YOUR HEART

The LORD their God will save them on that day
   as the flock of his people.
They will sparkle in his land
   like jewels in a crown.
How attractive and beautiful they will be!
                                        —ZECHARIAH (9:16–17)

Those who look to him are radiant;
   their faces are never covered with shame.
                                        —KING DAVID (PS. 34:5)

"Have you no other daughters?" "No," said the man. "There is a little stunted kitchen wench which my late wife left behind her, but she cannot be the bride." The King's son said he was to send her up to him; but the step-mother answered, "Oh no, she is much too dirty, she cannot show herself!" But he absolutely insisted on it, and Cinderella had to be called. She first washed her hands and face clean, and then went and bowed down before the King's son, who gave her the golden slipper. Then she seated herself on a stool, drew her foot out of the heavy wooden shoe, and put it into the slipper, which fit like a glove. And when she rose up and the King's son looked at her face, he recognized the beautiful maiden who had danced with him and cried, "This is the true bride!" The step-mother and two sisters were horrified and became pale with rage; he, however, took Cinderella on his horse and rode away with her.

I love this part of the story—to see the heroine unveiled in all her glory. To have her, *finally,* rise up to her full height. Mocked, hated, laughed at, spit upon—Cinderella is the one the slipper fits; she's the one the prince is in love with; *she's* the true bride. Just as we are. We, the ransomed church, are the bride of the King's Son, are we not? "Come, I will show you the bride, the wife of the Lamb" (Rev. 21:9). We've been chosen by him. We are the object of his love. "You have stolen my heart with one glance of your eyes" (Song 4:9). This fairy tale is *true.* I love it that in this passage from the original "Cinderella," the king's son *insisted* she come out of hiding. Though her family would keep her in the cellar, he'll have none of that. Come out. You are mine now. Let your light shine before men.

Still, if I'm honest, I appreciate the story . . . from a distance. The thought of *me* being called out of hiding is unnerving. I don't think I want to be seen. Many years ago, during my life in the theater, I received a standing ovation for a performance. The audience was literally on its feet, cheering. What actor doesn't crave a standing ovation? So you know what I did? I *ran.* Literally. As soon as the curtain went down I bolted for the door, so I wouldn't have to talk to anyone. I didn't want to be seen. I know, it's weird, but I'll bet you feel the same about being unveiled.

You probably can't imagine there being a glory to your life, let alone one that the Enemy fears. But remember—things are not what they seem. *We* are not what we seem. You probably believed that your heart was bad too. I pray that fog of poison gas from the pit of hell is fading away in the wind of God's truth. And there is more. Not only does Christ say to you that your heart is good, he invites you now out of the shadows to unveil your glory. You have a role you never dreamed of having.

There's the beautiful scene toward the end of Joseph's life where he, too, is unveiled. The very brothers who sold him into slavery as a boy are standing before what they believe is an angry Egyptian lord, equal in power to Pharaoh himself, their knees knocking. The silver cup of this dreaded lord was found stashed away in their luggage as they headed out of town—placed there by Joseph himself as a ruse. Now Joseph interrogates them till they squirm, deepening the plot by using an interpreter as if he doesn't understand Hebrew, pressing them hard. Finally, unable to hold back his tears, he *reveals* himself: "I am Joseph; does my father still live? . . . So you shall tell my father of all my glory in Egypt . . . and you shall hurry and bring my father down here" (Gen. 45:3, 13 NKJV). This is who I really am! Tell him about my glory! Amazing.

Much to everyone's surprise, Peter is unveiled at pentecost with quite a sermon that brings three thousand converts into the church. This from the man who denied Christ, three times, in his hour of need. Peter's buddies had to have been thinking, *Whoa, where did that come from?* And of course, Jesus himself, the carpenter's son, is unveiled on the Mount of Transfiguration for who he really is—the King of glory. In a beautiful mythic parallel, Aragorn, son of Arathorn and true heir to the throne of Gondor, is finally unveiled in the third book of Tolkien's trilogy, aptly titled *The Return of the King*. For years upon end he's merely been known as Strider, a Ranger, living out in the wilds doing no one really knows what. (Can anything good come out of *Nazareth*?) The chief of the Dunedain, the last great king of the race of men, Aragorn comes forward to take his rightful place.

Thus came Aragorn son of Arathorn, Elessar, Isildur's heir, out of the Paths of the Dead, borne upon a wind from the Sea to the kingdom of Gondor; and the mirth of the Rohirrim was a torrent of laughter and a flashing of swords, and the joy and wonder of the City was a music of trumpets and a ringing of bells. But the hosts of Mordor were seized with bewilderment, and a great wizardry it seemed to them that their own ships should be filled with their foes; and a black dread fell on them, knowing that the tides of fate had turned against them and their doom was at hand . . . But before all went Aragorn with the Flame of the West, Andúril like a new fire kindled, Narsil re-forged as deadly as of old; and upon his brow was the Star of Elendil.

The day has come, and the Morning Star has risen, never to set again. This unveiling, this coming into your glory, this is inevitable for the ransomed heart. If you'll recall, Moses put a veil over his face. That, too, was a picture of a deeper reality. We all do that. We have all veiled our glory, or someone has veiled it for us. Usually, some combination of both. But the time has come to set all veils aside:

> Now if the ministry that brought death, which was engraved in letters on stone, came with glory, so that the Israelites could not look steadily at the face of Moses because of its glory, fading though it was, will not the ministry of the Spirit be even more glorious? . . . Therefore, since we have such a hope, we are very bold. We are not like Moses, who would put a veil over his face to keep the Israelites from gazing at it while the radiance was fading away . . . And we, who with unveiled faces all reflect the Lord's glory, are being transformed into his likeness with ever-increasing glory, which comes from the Lord, who is the Spirit. (2 Cor. 3:7–8, 12–13, 18)

We are in the process of being unveiled. We were created to reflect God's glory, born to bear his image, and he ransomed us to reflect that glory again. Every heart was given a mythic glory, and that glory is being *restored*. Remember the mission of Christ: "I have come to give you back your heart and set you free." For as Saint Irenaeus said, "The glory of God is man fully alive." Certainly, you don't think the opposite is true. How do we bring God glory when we are sulking around in the cellar, weighed down by shame and guilt, hiding our light under a bushel? Our destiny is to come fully alive. To live with ever-*increasing* glory. This is the Third Eternal Truth every good myth has been trying to get across to us: *your heart bears a glory, and your glory is needed* . . . now. This is our desperate hour.

NO GOOD THING?

In an attempt to explain the biblical doctrine of sin, we've let something else creep in. You'll hear it come up almost automatically whenever Christians talk about themselves: "I'm just a sinner, saved by grace." "I'm just clothes for God to put on." "There sure isn't any good thing in me." It's so common this mind-set, this idea that we are no-good wretches, ready to sin at a moment's notice, incapable of goodness, and certainly far from any glory.

It's also unbiblical.

The passage people think they are referring to is Romans 7:18, where Paul says, "For I know that in me (that is, in my flesh,) dwelleth no good thing" (KJV). Notice the distinction he makes. He does *not* say, "There is nothing good in me. Period." What he says is that "*in my flesh* dwelleth no good thing." The flesh is the old nature, the old life, crucified with Christ. The flesh is the very thing God removed from our hearts when he circumcised them by his Spirit. In Galatians Paul goes on to explain, "Those who belong to

Christ Jesus have crucified the sinful nature [the flesh] with its passions and desires" (5:24). He does *not* say, "I am incapable of good." He says, "*In my flesh* dwelleth no good thing." In fact, just a few moments later, he discovers that "the law of the Spirit of life in Christ Jesus has made me free from the law of sin and death" (Rom. 8:2 NKJV).

Yes, we still battle with sin. *Yes,* we still have to crucify our flesh on a daily basis. "For if you live according to the flesh you will die; but if by the Spirit you put to death the deeds of the [sinful nature], you will live" (Rom. 8:13 NKJV). We have to *choose* to live from the new heart, and our old nature doesn't go down without a fight. I'll say more about that later. For now the question on the table is: Does the Bible teach that Christians are nothing but sinners—that there is nothing good in us? The answer is *no!* You have a new heart. Your heart is good. That sinful nature you battle *is not who you are.* Twice, in the famous chapter of Romans 7, where Paul presents a first-person angst about our battle against sin, he says, "But this is not my true nature. This is not my heart."

> As it is, *it is no longer I myself* who do it, but it is sin living in me. I know that nothing good lives in me, that is, in my sinful nature . . . Now if I do what I do not want to do, *it is no longer I* who do it, but it is sin living in me that does it . . . For in my inner being I delight in God's law. (vv. 17–18, 20, 22, emphasis added)

Paul is making a crucial distinction: *This is not me; this is not my true heart.* Listen to how he talks about himself in other places. He opens every letter by introducing himself as "Paul, an apostle." Not as a sinner, but as an apostle, writing to "the saints." Dump the religiosity; think about this *mythically.* Paul, appointed as a Great One in the kingdom, writing other Great Allies of the kingdom. How bold of him. There is no false humility, no groveling. He says,

Surely you have heard about the . . . grace that was given to me for you, that is, the mystery made known to me by revelation, as I have already written briefly. In reading this, then, you will be able to understand my insight into the mystery of Christ, which was not made known to men in other generations as it has now been revealed [to me]. (Eph. 3:2–5)

Paul is unashamed to say that he knows things no man before him knew. He even assumes they've heard about him, the mysteries revealed to him. That is part of his glory. His humility comes through clearly, in that he quickly admits that it's all been a gift, and in fact, a gift given to him *for others*.

And listen to the way he talks about us: "You shine like stars in the universe as you hold out the word of life" (Phil. 2:15–16). As Shawn Mullins sings, "we're born to shimmer; we're born to shine." You are *supposed* to shimmer. "Let your light shine before men" (Matt. 5:16). All this groveling and self-deprecation done by Christians is often just shame masquerading as humility. Shame says, "I'm nothing to look at. I'm not capable of goodness." Humility says, "I bear a glory for sure, but it is a *reflected* glory. A grace given to me." Your story does not begin with sin. It begins with a glory bestowed upon you by God. It does not start in Genesis 3; it starts in Genesis 1. First things first, as they say.

Certainly, you will admit that God is glorious. Is there anyone more kind? Is there anyone more creative? Is there anyone more valiant? Is there anyone more true? Is there anyone more daring? Is there anyone more beautiful? Is there anyone more wise? Is there anyone more generous? You are his offspring. His child. His reflection. His likeness. You bear *his* image. Do remember that though he made the heavens and the earth in all their glory, the desert and the open sea, the meadow and the Milky Way, and said, "It is good," it was only *after* he made you that he said, "It is *very* good"

(Gen. 1:31). Think of it: your original glory was greater than anything that's ever taken your breath away in nature.

> As for the saints who are in the land,
>> they are the glorious ones in whom is all my delight. (Ps. 16:3)

God endowed you with a glory when he created you, a glory so deep and mythic that all creation pales in comparison. A glory unique to you, just as your fingerprints are unique to you, just as the way you laugh is unique to you. Somewhere down deep inside we've been looking for that glory ever since. A man wants to know that he is truly a man, that he could be brave; he longs to know that he is a warrior; and all his life he wonders, "Have I got what it takes?" A woman wants to know that she is truly a woman, that she is beautiful; she longs to know that she is captivating; and all her life she wonders, "Do I have a beauty to offer?" The poet Yeats wrote,

> If I make the lashes dark
> And the eyes more bright
> And the lips more scarlet,
> Or ask if all be right
> From mirror after mirror
> No vanity's displayed:
> I'm looking for the face I had
> Before the world was made.
> ("Before the World Was Made" from the poem "A Woman Young and Old")

Yes, that's it. When you take a second glance in the mirror, when you pause to look again at a photograph, you are looking for a glory you know you were meant to have, if only because you know you long to have it. You remember faintly that you were once more than what you have become. Your story didn't start with sin, and thank God, it does not end with sin. It ends with glory restored: "Those he justified, he also glorified" (Rom. 8:30). And "in the meantime," you have *been* transformed, and you are *being* transformed. You've been given a new heart. Now God is restoring your glory. He is bringing you fully alive. Because the glory of God is you fully alive.

UNDER A SPELL

"Well, then, if this is all true, why don't I see it?" Precisely. Exactly. Now we are reaching my point. The fact that you do not see your good heart and your glory is only proof of how effective the assault has been. We don't see ourselves clearly. Have you forgotten your fairy tales?

In *The Silver Chair* (the sixth story of the Narnia series), two English schoolchildren—Eustace and Jill—are summoned into Narnia to find the missing crown prince of that kingdom. Years earlier Prince Rilian was abducted by a witch, placed under a spell, and taken to her underground kingdom. Once a day, for an hour, the prince would wake from the magic spell and realize where he was and *who* he was and what had happened. But during those hours he was chained to a silver chair so that he could not escape. All the other hours of the day he was "free" because he was convinced that the witch was good and he was her grateful slave, a no-good wretch. Near the climax of the story the children—with the help of Puddleglum the Marsh-wiggle—free the prince from the chair and the power of the spell.

> Then he turned and surveyed his rescuers; and the something wrong, whatever it was, had vanished from his face. "What?" he cried, turning to Puddleglum. "Do I see before me a Marsh-wiggle—a real, live, honest, Narnian Marsh-wiggle?" "Oh, so you

have heard of Narnia, after all?" said Jill. "Had I forgotten it when I was under the spell?" asked the Knight. "Well, that and all other bedevilments are now over. You may well believe that I know Narnia, for I am Rilian, Prince of Narnia, and Caspian the great King is my Father." "Your Royal Highness," said Puddleglum, sinking on one knee (and the children did the same), "we have come hither for no other end than to seek you."

"How long then have I been in the power of the witch?" "It is more than ten years since your Highness was lost in the woods at the north side of Narnia." "Ten years!" said the Prince, drawing his hand across his face as if to rub away the past. "Yes, I believe you. For now that I am myself I can remember that enchanted life, though while I was enchanted I could not remember my true self."

"Though while I was enchanted I could not remember my true self." That's it exactly. We are under a spell. We are alert and oriented times zero. We have no idea who we really are. Whatever glory was bestowed, whatever glory is being restored, we thought this whole Christian thing was about . . . something else. Trying not to sin. Going to church. Being nice. Jesus says it is about healing your heart, setting it free, restoring your glory. A religious fog has tried to veil all that, put us under some sort of spell or amnesia, to keep us from coming alive. Pascal said, "It is a monstrous thing . . . an incomprehensible enchantment, and a supernatural slumber." And Paul said, It is time to take that veil away.

Whenever anyone turns to the Lord, the veil is taken away. Now the Lord is the Spirit, and where the Spirit of the Lord is, there is freedom. And we, who with unveiled faces all reflect the Lord's glory, are being transformed into his likeness with ever-increasing glory, which comes from the Lord, who is the Spirit. (2 Cor. 3:16–18)

A veil removed, bringing freedom, transformation, glory. Do you see it? I am not making this up—though I have been accused of making the gospel better than it is. The charge is laughable. Could anyone be more generous than God? Could any of us come up with a story that beats the one God has come up with? All the stories that we tell borrow their power from the Great Story he is telling. Take the movie *The Lion King*, ignore the "circle of life" stuff—the whole myth is borrowed from Christianity. There once was a beautiful kingdom. But it was stolen by the evil one. Its glory has been marred. Badly. Now it's time for the true king to come back and take over. But Simba—the lion heir to the throne—doesn't believe who he is. His father was murdered when he was young, and the enemy blamed it on Simba. Simba ran away, and after years of losing heart, he winds up living with a wart hog and a meerkat whose highest ambitions in life are breakfast, lunch, and dinner. Then, one night, Simba's father appears to him in a vision:

MUFASA: Simba.

SIMBA: Father?

MUFASA: Simba, you have forgotten me.

SIMBA: No! How could I?

MUFASA: You have forgotten who you are, and so forgotten me. Look inside yourself, Simba . . . you are more than what you have become.

SIMBA: How can I go back? I'm not who I used to be.

MUFASA: Remember who you are. You are my son, and the one true king. Remember who you are.

Simba finally throws off the veil of shame and self-reproach and goes back to take the kingdom that is rightly his. As a result, his glory and the glory of the realm are restored. Something similar happens toward the end of *The Matrix*. Neo joins the forces seeking to set the world free. He has left behind the identity of Thomas Anderson, computer guy, nobody special really. He's taken many risks, lived by faith. But the real moment of his glory comes when he finally turns to face his enemy. Up to this point everyone has run from the "agents," who are symbols of the demonic. John writes in his first epistle, "You, dear children, are from God and have overcome them, because the one who is in you is greater than the one who is in the world . . . The whole world is under the control of the evil one" (1 John 4:4; 5:19). No one has challenged them; no one has taken them on. As Neo turns to confront evil incarnate, his friends are watching, incredulous, afraid.

> TRINITY: What's he doing?
> MORPHEUS: He's beginning to believe.

What is he beginning to believe? *Who he really is.*

YOUR TRUEST SELF

Then from on high—somewhere in the distance
There's a voice that calls—remember who you are
If you lose yourself—your courage soon will follow
So be strong tonight—remember who you are
(Gavin Greenaway and Trevor Horn, *Sound the Bugle*)

You are going to need your whole heart in all its glory for this Story you've fallen into. You'll need every ounce of courage and faith and love you can muster. So, who did God mean when he meant you? We at least know this: we know that we are not what we were meant to be. Most of us spend our energy trying to hide that fact, through all the veils we put on and the false selves we create. Our first parents thought they could hide behind fig leaves and in the bushes, and we do the same—only with more sophistication. Far better to spend our energy trying to recover the image of God and unveil it for his glory. One means that will help us is any story that helps us see with the eyes of the heart. Which brings us back to myth. Poet David Whyte says, "Myths reveal to us what we are capable of." Clyde Kilby offers this image: "Myth is a lane down which we walk in order to repossess our soul." Wow! Wouldn't you love to repossess your soul? To live with an unmasked, unveiled glory that reflects the glory of the Lord? That's worth fighting for.

The Bible is filled with characters—I don't mean people playing parts; I mean the word your grandmother uses for your grandfather, who at the age of eighty-seven just got himself his fourth speeding ticket in a month. "He's a real character." Or as you say of those folks who wear hats or sing loud or walk to the beat of a drummer nobody else is hearing. Abraham is a character; so is his wife, Sarah. King David is a character. The disciples of Jesus are all characters. Take James and John, for instance, "the sons of Zebedee." You might remember them as the ones who cornered Jesus to angle for the choice seats at his right and left hands in the kingdom. Or the time they wanted to call down fire from heaven to destroy a village that wouldn't offer Jesus a place for the night. Their buddies call them idiots; Jesus calls them the Sons of Thunder (Mark 3:17). He sees who they *really* are. It's their mythic name, their true identity. They look like fishermen out of work; they are actually the Sons of Thunder.

There are stories that you've loved; there are characters that you've resonated with down deep inside, maybe even dreamed that you could be. Do you know why? Deep is calling unto deep. They spoke to you—they speak even now—because they contain some hint or glimpse into your true self. My friend Bethann paused, then said, "Really? Could it really be that there is a hidden greatness in me?" Myth is how we discover it. Rolland Hein explains, "Whether or not people are aware of the fact, they cannot live without myth, nor can they reach full stature as people without true myths."

WHAT OUR MYTHS REVEAL

Taped across the top of my computer, just above the screen on which I am now typing this sentence, I've pasted another: "*Ego numquam pronunciare mendacium, sed ego sum homo indomitus.*" It's Latin, for those of you, like me, who don't know their Latin, a line from the movie *Braveheart.* Translated, it means "I never tell lies, but I am a savage." And there's a lot of story behind it. Personal myth. Like all stories, this one starts way back in my youth. As a young boy, I used to make up lies about myself because I didn't think there was anything special or worthy about the real me. I told my friends I was part Indian, or a robber by night, or a motorcycle racer. I made up a glory because I was convinced I had none of my own.

Fast-forward to last summer when I led a group of friends into the Wimunche Wilderness on a backpacking expedition. We were on a sort of mission. *Wild at Heart* (a book I wrote about men recovering their masculine soul) had just come out that spring, and we were sort of living it out each day. In the morning, I'd suggest a question to wrestle with, pray about as we sweated our way through the wilderness. After dinner in the evening, we'd share our thoughts and stories around the campfire, and so we processed our lives against the book. Or vice versa. On the fourth day of the trip, as we broke camp in the woods near Twin Lakes, I suggested that the issue for the day was simply this: God, who am I? What do you think of me? What's my real name?

This was The Question, the coveted question, the one we all wanted to ask on day one but knew it wouldn't come until we'd wrestled with other business, like the father wound and the role of the Woman in our lives. We had to sort of earn the right to ask this question, and after what we'd been through the day before, it seemed we'd paid our dues. (We'd lost the trail and took a three-mile detour through dense, leg-thrashing, face-lashing willows, which the elk seemed to have no trouble penetrating until I realized their legs are two feet longer than ours. We took the whole mess head-on for hours under the afternoon sun.)

Now, the day after, hoisting our packs, we headed out to cross a high pass and then down a long valley to another unknown camp. It started raining about ten minutes later, and the wind really whipped up as we climbed above the tree line. All was wetness and heather and rock and crag . . . and I was *loving* it. It reminded me of the Scottish Highlands in *Braveheart;* I felt I was hiking in a mythic reality. Then I remembered the day's mission, and I began to ask God one of the most important questions any of us will ever ask: *What do you think of me, God? Who am I to you?* The guys were strung out over a mile or two along the trail by now, and I was alone and just reaching the pass.

You are my Wallace.

Something in my heart sank. Yes, sank. *Good grief, John—look at you. You're pathetic. You're making up the voice of God. Filling in the blanks. Cooking up what you'd want him to say.* Whether or not it was the voice of God, it took only about ten seconds to shut it down with a generous dose of heartache for wanting to hear something like this ever since I was young, and contempt for thinking I'd stepped in for God to pronounce the name, and self-reproach for not being willing to just hike awhile in silence and let God speak for himself. At about this point some of the guys caught up to me, and we stopped to snap a few photos at the pass. Then we headed down.

We reached camp with about an hour to spare before the dinner chores, so I took a walk by myself out into the meadow. No, that's not exactly right. I left camp because I felt *summoned*. I knew God was waiting for me, there at the end of the day, just like a father or a friend, unwilling to let the matter slip away. As I began to tune in to my heart once more, I heard him ask me a question. (Just so you don't think I'm schizophrenic, entertaining voices, let me remind you that the heart has become the new dwelling place of God, and it is in the heart that we hear his voice. I'll say more on that in a minute.) God's question to me felt unrelated to the event at the pass.

> *Tell me what you love.*
>
> *Oh. Well . . . I loved the hike this morning. The wind and the rain and wildness of it all. The Highlands.* [Did I just say *Highlands*?]
>
> *Go on.*
>
> *Well, I love this sort of expedition too. I love leading a band of men.*
>
> *Is there anything else?* [Each question felt like it was taking me deeper into my own heart.]
>
> *I love fighting for people's freedom.*
>
> There was a moment of silence.
>
> *Are you convinced?*

God took me into the truth of the mythic name through the doorway of my own heart and my desires. I was trapped; there was no denying now that it was God who spoke that morning. I was forced to wrestle with the fact that what he spoke was true. Over the past year I have needed that mythic name and all the strength and courage it offers. The battle has been ugly, and there are many hearts to free. The Accuser laughs and mocks and throws everything he can: "You are making this up. You are a weak little man." *Ego numquam pronunciare mendacium, sed ego sum homo indomitus.* I never tell lies, but I am a savage.

EMBRACING THE GLORY

Our deepest fear is not that we are inadequate. Our deepest fear is that we are powerful beyond measure. It is our light, not our darkness, that most frightens us. We ask ourselves, "Who am I to be brilliant, gorgeous, talented and fabulous?" Actually, who are you not to be? You are a child of God. Your playing small doesn't serve the world. There's nothing enlightened about shrinking so that other people won't feel insecure around you. We were born to manifest the glory of God that is within us . . . And as we let our own light shine, we unconsciously give other people permission to do the same. As we are liberated from our own fear, our presence automatically liberates others. (Nelson Mandela)

When I first read this quote, I thought, *No, that's not true*. We don't fear our glory. We fear we are not glorious at all. We fear that at bottom, we are going to be revealed as . . . disappointments. Mandela is just trying to make a nice speech, like a sermon, to buoy us up for a day or two. But as I thought about it more, I realized we *do* fear our glory. We fear even heading this direction because, for one thing, it seems prideful. Now pride is a bad thing, to be sure, but it's not prideful to embrace the truth that you bear the image of God. Paul says it brings glory to God. We walk in humility because we know it is a glory *bestowed*. It reflects something of the Lord's glory.

The deeper reason we fear our own glory is that once we let others see it, they will have seen the truest us, and that is nakedness indeed. We can repent of our sin. We can work on our "issues." But there is nothing to be "done" about our glory. It's so naked. It's just there—the truest us. It is an awkward thing to shimmer when everyone else around you is not, to walk in your glory with an unveiled face when everyone else is veiling his. For a woman to be truly feminine and beautiful is to invite suspicion, jealousy, mis-understanding. A friend confided in me, "When you walk into a room, every woman looks at you to see—are you prettier than they are? Are you a threat?"

And that is why living from your glory is the only loving thing to do. You cannot love another person from a false self. You cannot love another while you are still hiding. How can you help them to freedom while you remain captive? You cannot love another unless you offer her your heart. It takes courage to live from your heart. My friend Jenny said just the other day, "I desperately want to be who I am. I don't want the glory that I marvel at in others anymore. I want to be that glory which God set in me."

Finally, our deepest fear of all . . . we will need to live from it. To admit we do have a new heart and a glory from God, to begin to let it be unveiled and embrace it as true—that means the next thing God will do is ask us to live from it. Come out of the boat. Take the throne. Be what he meant us to be. And that feels risky . . . really risky. But it is also exciting. It is coming fully alive. My friend Morgan declared, "It's a risk worth taking."

> But I can cry—
> O Enemy, the maker hath not done;
> One day thou shalt behold, and from the sight wilt run.
> (George MacDonald)

PART THREE

THE FOUR STREAMS

Did you feel the darkness tremble?
When all the saints joined in one song
And all the streams flow as one river
To wash away our brokenness.
—MARTIN SMITH, "DID YOU FEEL
THE MOUNTAINS TREMBLE?"

From Eden a river flowed to water the park, which on leaving the park branched into four streams.
—GENESIS 2:10 (MOFFATT)

In the Garden known as Eden there was a spring. Issuing from the depths of the earth, this fount became the headwaters of a mighty river, which in turn parted into four great streams. Saint Bonaventure saw in that a foreshadowing, a mythic symbol of "an ever-flowing fountain," as he called it, "that becomes a great and living river with four channels to water the garden of the entire Church." I think if you will look again at the ways in which Christ ransoms people, the *means* by which he makes a man or a woman come fully alive, you'll find he offers his life to us through Four

Streams. Those streams are Discipleship, Counseling, Healing, and Warfare.

The *terms* might sound familiar; but for so many of us they are familiar in the way that we've heard Saturn has rings around it or that Antarctica is a frozen continent. Our actual *experience* of the Four Streams is not what it could be . . . if it were, we would be "the glorious ones" by now (Ps. 16:3). It will help to think of them as walking with God, Receiving God's Intimate Counsel, Deep Restoration, and Spiritual Warfare.

Long have these streams been separated. I imagine we've sipped from only one or two. Now is the time for them to flow together again. That is how our glory is restored, how we find the life Christ offers, how we live in his Story. To discover for yourself that the glory of God *is* man fully alive, you must drink deeply from the Four Streams that Christ sends to you.

CHAPTER SIX

WALKING WITH GOD

Narrow the road that leads to life, and only a few find it.

—JESUS (MATT. 7:14)

You have made known to me the path of life.

—KING DAVID (PS. 16:11)

After the Road had run down some way, and had left Bree-hill standing tall and brown behind, they came on a narrow track that led off towards the North. "This is where we leave the open road and take to cover," said Strider.

"Not a 'short cut' I hope," said Pippin. "Our last short cut through woods nearly ended in disaster."

"Ah, but you had not got me with you then," laughed Strider. "My cuts, short or long, don't go wrong." He took a look up and down the Road. No one was in sight; and he led the way quickly down towards the wooded valley . . .

Strider guided them confidently among the many crossing paths, although left to themselves they would soon have been at a loss. He was taking a wandering course with many turns and doublings, to put off any pursuit . . . Whether because of Strider's skill or for some other reason, they saw no sign and heard no sound of any other living thing all that day . . .

They had not gone far on the fifth day when they left the last straggling pools and reed-beds of the marshes behind them. The land before them began steadily to rise again. Away in the distance eastward they could now see a line of hills. The highest of them was at the right of the line and a little separated from the others. It had a conical top, slightly flattened at the summit. "That is Weathertop," said Strider . . .

They stood for a while silent on the hill-top, near its southern edge. In that lonely place Frodo for the first time fully realized his homelessness and danger. He wished bitterly that his fortune had left him in the quiet and beloved Shire. He stared down at the hateful Road, leading back westward—to his home. Suddenly he was aware that two black specks were moving slowly along it, going westward; and looking again he saw that three others were creeping eastward to meet them. He gave a cry and clutched Strider's arm. "Look," he said, pointing downwards. At once Strider flung himself on the ground behind the ruined circle, pulling Frodo down beside him. Merry threw himself alongside.

Slowly they crawled up to the edge of the ring again, and peered through a cleft between two jagged stones. The light was no longer bright, for the clear morning had faded . . . neither Frodo nor Merry could make out their shapes for certain; yet something told them that there, far below, were Black Riders assembling on the Road beyond the foot of the hill. "Yes," said Strider, whose keener sight left him in no doubt. "The enemy is here!" (J. R. R. Tolkien, *The Fellowship of the Ring*)

GUIDED

I was downstairs early one Tuesday morning in September, a cold and foggy morning, with a blanket wrapped around me as I read, trying to capture some moments with God before the whirlwind of the day swept upon me, when I came across a passage on forgiveness. Now, I think you'll know what I mean when I say it seemed to "speak" louder or more clearly than everything else I had been reading. I could not pass on. I tried to, but I sensed that the Spirit of God was saying, *Go back to that passage—linger there.* I tried to read ahead . . . but everything after was stale. I went back and read the passage over. There it was again, that tang, that prompt, that sense of *This is what I want you to pay attention to.* The passage was warning about the dangers of an unforgiving heart, how damaging it can be.

> *Am I an unforgiving person, Lord? Is that what you are trying to say?*

> *No . . . I am warning you. Remember this. You are going to need to be forgiving.*

In less than an hour I received a phone call that can only be described in terms of Betrayal. It was devastating. Some allies we had asked to help us with a project very dear to us announced they were quitting—changing horses midstream, walking away from the battle just as it was getting hot. I was stunned, speechless. It was so out of the blue, so *unlike* them, I did not know what to say. The injury was doubled by an attempt to fix the blame on us; it was because of *our* attitudes that they had chosen to abandon ship.

Dumbfounded, blindsided, I knew this much: *This cannot bring happiness to God.* I asked if there was any way to make amends. No. Was there anything we could do to patch things up? No. As I probed the matter further, earnestly seeking a way to rebuild the friendship, their story grew increasingly thin and contradictory. They were walking away. Period. And it was *our* fault.

As the news settled in, I wanted to get angry. I was hurt. Run through with a sword. Then, like some wolf in the night sniffing at my door, I could feel Resentment trying to get in. After all, it seemed a completely justifiable response. Just as I was lifting the latch, I remembered the Lord's warning. *Oh . . . this is what you meant. Forgive.* I barred the door, refused to let Resentment in. Ten minutes later, as our conversation continued the way of the Paris Peace Talks, something else came scrounging for admittance; I was tempted to turn to Self-Reproach. Even though I really didn't think we'd done anything to earn such a betrayal, I was willing to own it nonetheless. *No . . . this is not your fault. Simply forgive them.* After more than an hour, the conversation was clearly at an impasse. Their position was making me madder than ever; I wanted to go to Pride. We were clearly in the right. *No, do not turn to Pride. Simply forgive them.*

I hung up the phone, exhausted. Then I had to call a number of closely involved parties and do my best to give a gracious and impartial account of what happened, trying to honor their stated reasons, trying to own our part in the divorce. Each new conversation brought another round of emotion: Betrayal, and with it Anger, Hurt, Resentment, Indignation, False Guilt—the whole nasty menagerie, like a pack of hungry coyotes circling the camp. *Simply forgive them.* Bar the door. Every other emotion, every other reaction felt dangerous, loaded with some further evil. Falling into bed that night, I felt as though I'd been guided by some wise Ranger like Aragorn through a dark forest, with a hundred wrong turns at every side. I felt *rescued.*

My journals are full of such stories. There must be hundreds, maybe close to a thousand by now. God has gotten me out of all sorts of tight spots—saved my life more than once, literally. He's also guided me into all sorts of beautiful surprises and adventures.

Now, it could be that I'm just a slow learner, and God is being specially gracious to a man who needs a little extra help. Lord knows, I do. But I don't think he speaks to me any more than others; I think I've just learned to expect it, need it, keep an eye out for it. It's a whole different perspective on how we approach our day. Either we wake to tackle our "to do" list, get things done, guided by our morals and whatever clarity we may at the moment have (both rather lacking to the need, I might add). Or we wake in the midst of a dangerous Story, as God's intimate ally, following him into the unknown.

If you're not pursuing a dangerous quest with your life, well, then, you don't need a Guide. If you haven't found yourself in the midst of a ferocious war, then you won't need a seasoned Captain. If you've settled in your mind to live as though this is a fairly neutral world and you are simply trying to live your life as best you can, then you can probably get by with the Christianity of tips and techniques. Maybe. I'll give you about a fifty-fifty chance. But if you intend to live in the Story that God is telling, and if you want the life he offers, then you are going to need more than a handful of principles, however noble they may be. There are too many twists and turns in the road ahead, too many ambushes waiting only God knows where, too much at stake. You cannot possibly prepare yourself for every situation. Narrow is the way, said Jesus. How shall we be sure to find it? We need God intimately, and we need him desperately.

"You have made known to me the path of life," David said (Ps. 16:11). Yes—that's it. In all the ins and outs of this thing we call living, there is one narrow path to life, and we need help finding it.

What Is Discipleship?

On the other hand, there is what we have come to accept as discipleship. A friend of mine recently handed me a program from a large and successful church somewhere in the Midwest. It's a rather exemplary model of what the idea has fallen to. Their plan for discipleship involves, first, becoming a member of this particular church. Then they encourage you to take a course on doctrine. Be "faithful" in attending the Sunday morning service and a small group fellowship. Complete a special course on Christian growth. Live a life that demonstrates clear evidence of spiritual growth. Complete a class on evangelism. Consistently look for opportunities to evangelize. Complete a course on finances, one on marriage, and another on parenting (provided that you are married or a parent). Complete a leadership training course, a hermeneutics course, a course on spiritual gifts, and another on biblical counseling. Participate in missions. Carry a significant local church ministry "load."

You're probably surprised that I would question this sort of program; most churches are trying to get their folks to complete something like this, one way or another. No doubt a great deal of helpful information is passed on. My goodness, you could earn an MBA with less effort. But let me ask you: A program like this—does it teach a person how to apply principles, or how to walk with God? They are not the same thing. Change the content and any cult could do this. I mean, Gandhi was a remarkable man; so was Lao-tzu, Confucius, or Thomas Jefferson. They all had *principles* for a better life. But only Christianity can teach you to walk with God.

We forfeit that birthright when we take folks through a discipleship program whereby they master any number of Christian precepts and miss the most important thing of all, the very thing for which we were created: intimacy with God. There are, after all, those troubling words Jesus spoke to those who were doing all the "right" things: "Then I will tell them plainly, 'I never knew you'" (Matt 7:23). Knowing God. That's the point.

You might recall the old proverb: "Give a man a fish and you feed him for a day; teach a man to fish and you feed him for a lifetime." The same holds true here. Teach a man a rule and you help him solve a problem; teach a man to walk with God and you help him solve the rest of his life. Truth be told, you couldn't master enough principles to see you safely through this Story. There are too many surprises, ambiguities, exceptions to the rule. Things are hard at work—is it time to make a move? What *has* God called you to do with your life? Things are hard at home—is this just a phase your son is going through, or should you be more concerned? You can't seem to shake this depression—is it medical or something darker? What does the future hold for you—and how should you respond?

Only by walking with God can we hope to find the path that leads to life. *That* is what it means to be a disciple. After all—aren't we "followers of Christ"? Then by all means, let's actually *follow* him. Not ideas about him. Not just his principles. Him.

By Wisdom

A personal walk with God comes to us through wisdom and revelation. You will soon discover that we need both.

> For a moment the King's grief and anger were so great that he could not speak. Then he said: "Come, friends. We must go up river and find the villains who have done this, with all the speed we may. I will not leave one of them alive." "Sire, with a good will," said Jewel. But Roonwit said, "Sire, be wary in your just wrath. There are strange doings on foot. If there should be rebels in arms further up the valley, we three are too few to meet them. If it would please you to wait while . . ." "I will not wait the tenth part of a second," said the King. "But while Jewel and I go forward, do you gallop as hard as you may to Cair Paravel . . . we must go on and take the adventure that comes to us." "It is the only thing left for us to do, Sire," said the Unicorn. He did not see at the moment how foolish it was for two of them to go on alone; nor did the

King. They were too angry to think clearly. But much evil came
of their rashness in the end. (C. S. Lewis, *The Last Battle*)

King Tirian of Narnia has a good heart. But he also has an
unwise heart—an untrained heart. I'd say that's true for most of us.
Our heart has been made good by the work of Christ, but we
haven't learned how to live from it. Young and naive it remains. It's
as though we've been handed a golden harp or a shining sword.
Even the most gifted musician still has to take lessons; even the
bravest of warriors must be trained. We are unfamiliar, unpracticed
with the ways of the heart. This is actually a very dangerous part of
the journey. Launching out with an untrained heart can bring
much hurt and ruin, and afterward we will be shamed back into the
gospel of Sin Management, having concluded that our heart is
bad. It isn't bad; it's just young and unwise. The poet George
Herbert warned,

> Go not abroad at every quest or call
>   of an untrained hope or passion.

When the apostles needed the help of some good men to shepherd the exploding new church, they chose men "full of the Spirit
and wisdom" (Acts 6:3). The two go together; we need both. We
need to walk by the inspiration of the Spirit, and we need wisdom
as well. Wisdom and revelation. Early on in our journey, I think we
should lean more into wisdom. It takes time to learn to walk with
God in a deeply intimate way, and many challenges face us before
we are accustomed to the way of the heart. We must practice our
chords; we must do our drills.

> For the waywardness of the simple will kill them,
>   and the complacency of fools will destroy them;

but whoever listens to me will live in safety
>   and be at ease, without fear of harm . . .
Then you will understand what is right and just
>   and fair—every good path.
For wisdom will enter *your heart,*
>   and knowledge will be pleasant to your soul.
Discretion will protect you,
>   and understanding will guard you. (Prov. 1:32–33; 2:9–11,
emphasis added)

A friend of mine wanted to teach English as a second language in an Asian country as a way of becoming a sort of undercover missionary. A beautiful dream, one that I'm sure she would have been excellent in fulfilling. But she rushed to the field unprepared in many ways. I don't mean finances and language skills; I mean in the ways of the heart. Lurking down in her soul were some deep and unresolved issues that would set her up for a fall: among them shame and guilt from an abusive past. The team she joined was totally unfamiliar with the new heart, and they doubted its goodness; as with too many Christian ministries, shame and guilt were often used as motivators. Their old covenant theology would play right into Susan's issues, shut down her young heart. Finally, she was unpracticed in spiritual warfare, ill-equipped for what hell would throw at her. The devil is a master at shame and guilt. She went; she got hammered; she came home, defeated. Her friends wonder if she'll ever try it again.

The disaster could have been avoided. Wisdom was crying out: do not rush the field (Luke 14:31); train yourself to discern good and evil (Heb. 5:14); live as though your life is at stake, and the enemy is waiting to outwit you (Matt. 10:16). God has given us all sorts of counsel and direction in his written Word; thank God, we have it written down in black and white. We would do well to be familiar with it, study it with all the intensity of the men who studied the maps of the Normandy coastline before they hit the beaches on D-Day. The more that wisdom enters our hearts, the more we will be able to trust our hearts in difficult situations. Notice that wisdom is not cramming our heads with principles. It is developing a discerning *heart*. What made Solomon such a sharp guy was his wise and discerning heart (1 Kings 3:9).

We don't seek wisdom because it's a good idea; we seek wisdom because we're dead if we don't. We seek wisdom because the trail is narrow and hard to find. It is a cruel thing to tell someone to follow her dreams without also warning her what hell will come against her. High school and college commencement speeches are full of such naïveté. Reach for the stars; follow your dreams; find yourself. It's not that the advice is bad; it is, however, woefully inadequate. That's like a thirteen-year-old falling in love. Her motives may be lovely, but she is in for a painful fall. Will she ever love again with such abandon?

AND REVELATION

Wisdom is crucial. But wisdom is not enough. Many well-meaning evangelicals rely on it exclusively. That is why their lives remain where they are—rather short of all Christ promised. Okay—way short. Wisdom is essential . . . and insufficient.

Saul of Tarsus was headed to Damascus, "breathing out murderous threats against the Lord's disciples," with official documents granting him permission to arrest all Christians in the city and have them sent to prison (Acts 9:1–2). Now, you and I know that Jesus changed Saul's agenda radically before he ever reached the city—the blinding light, the voice from heaven, the total realignment of his worldview. But the believers in Damascus don't know all this. As they wait in fear for Saul's arrival, God speaks to one of them, a man named Ananias, and tells him to go to the house where Saul is staying, lay hands on him, and pray for him. Understandably, Ananias suggests this is not such a good idea: "Lord . . . I have heard many reports about this man and all the harm he has done to your saints in Jerusalem. And he has come here with authority from the chief priests to arrest all who call on your name" (9:13–14). It's okay, God says, he's my man now. Against wisdom Ananias goes, and the greatest of all the apostles is launched.

The Bible is full of such counterintuitive direction from God. Would you counsel a father to sacrifice his only child, the only hope for the promised nation? Certainly, it wasn't wisdom that compelled a fugitive to walk back into the country where he was wanted for murder, a land where all his kin were held as slaves, march into Pharaoh's palace and demand their release. Was it reasonable to take a fortified city by marching around it blowing trumpets? What's the sense of slashing the ranks of your army from 32,000 to 300, just before battle? It was dangerous advice, indeed, to send the young maiden before her king unbidden, and even worse to send a boy against a trained mercenary. And frankly, it looked like perfect madness for Jesus to give himself up to the authorities, let himself get killed.

Somewhere in our hearts I think we'd all love to have a role like that, be used by God so dramatically. To find it, wisdom is just not enough—may even hold us *back* from doing the will of God. The particular foolishness of the church in the past century was Reason above all else. The result has been a faith stripped of the supernatural, the Christianity of tips and techniques. The commonsense life, which, as Oswald Chambers warned, can be the enemy of the supernatural life. Many of the ministries and churches I've known made their decisions by principles and expedience. We have our morals and we have our precepts, but where is the living God? How will we hear him call us out of Ur, lead us to our own promised land, bring us through our own Calvary? Putting all our confidence in human reason was naive, and it left us in a very dangerous position. The only way out of this mess is to turn to our Guide, our Captain, to learn to walk with God.

REVELATION: LISTENING FOR HIS VOICE

We begin by assuming that God is still speaking.

An old hymn celebrating the wonderful Scriptures has a line that goes something like this: "What more can he say, than to you he has said?" The implication being that God has said all he has to say to us in the Bible. Period. It sounds orthodox. Except that's not what the Bible says: "I have much more to say to you, more than you can now bear. But when he, the Spirit of truth, comes, he will guide you into all truth" (John 16:12–13). There's more that Jesus wants to say to you, much more, and now that his Spirit resides in your heart, the conversation can continue. Many good people never hear God speak to them personally for the simple fact that they've never been told that he *does*. But he does—generously, intimately. "He who belongs to God hears what God says" (John 8:47).

> The man who enters by the gate is the shepherd of his sheep. The watchman opens the gate for him, and the sheep listen to his voice. He calls his own sheep by name and leads them out. When he has brought out all his own, he goes on ahead of them, and his sheep follow him because they know his voice . . . I am the good shepherd. (John 10:2–4, 11)

You don't just leave sheep to find their way in the world. They are famous for getting lost, attacked by wild animals, falling into some pit, and that is why they must stay close to the shepherd, follow his voice. And no shepherd could be called good unless he personally guided his flock through danger. But that is precisely what he promises to do. He *wants* to speak to you; he wants to lead you to good pasture. Now, it doesn't happen in an instant. Walking with God is a way of life. It's something to be learned; our ability to hear God's voice and discern his word to us grows over time. As Brother Lawrence had it, we "practice the presence of God." We have an eye out for his particular word to us, and we learn as we go along. At first Frodo wasn't sure he could trust Strider; some of his choices seemed unwise. Frodo said, "I was afraid of him at first . . . but I have become very fond of him."

Two years ago we spent a wonderful family vacation at a ranch here in Colorado—horseback riding, campfires, porch swings, home cookin'. It was one of the best weeks we'd had together in a long time. So when it came to making plans for this past summer, it seemed like a no-brainer. We just assumed we'd go back and do it again. Heck, it would be even *better* the second time around because we would be familiar with the place. And wouldn't it be neat to build a family tradition? But as we asked God about it, Stasi and I sensed him saying, *Not this year*. It was hard counsel to accept; everybody wanted to go back. Three times we asked God about it, and each time he said *No*. When the Hayman Fire burned 137,000 acres of Colorado in June, we looked at each other and realized that was the week we would have been at the ranch. It was almost totally engulfed in flames. He made known to us the path of life.

Notice that we must *ask*. And we will sometimes struggle *to* hear and struggle with *what* we hear. But personally, it's worth it. I'm after the path of life—and he alone knows it.

In fact, walking with God is how he led me into the Four Streams. I was sitting upstairs one Saturday morning, having some time with God, when he spoke to me two words: *Jack Hayford*. I paused, waiting to hear what the Lord wanted to say. That was it. Jack Hayford. I said, "Yes, Lord . . . anything else?" Silence. I sort of shrugged it off as my weirdness. A random thought. About an hour later, the phone rang. My friend Joni was calling from the lobby of a conference here in town.

"John, I know this is late notice and it's Saturday and all . . . but I think you're supposed to be at this conference . . . so I bought you a ticket."

I was silent. Truth is, I was bugged. This was my day off.

"Jack Hayford is speaking next," she added.

"I'll be right there."

It was a powerful and balanced talk Jack gave that day, on how we bring the life of Christ to people. As almost a side comment, he said, "All the streams are coming together now in the church—Healing, Counseling, Deliverance, and Discipleship." My heart leapt. *Yes. That's it! That's what we need in order to see people come alive—to see them set free.*

Let me share a more troubling example. In the fall of 2001 I was scheduled to take the gospel to Edinburgh, Scotland, and Dublin, Ireland. It was a mission I felt very called to, and I was very much looking forward to it. Stasi and the boys were coming along. Our flight plan had us departing on September 11. Several weeks beforehand we were impressed that we should leave earlier. As we prayed, we sensed God was saying, *Leave on the tenth.* Against all normal procedures, our agent was able to change our outbound flight. As you know, had we stayed with the eleventh, we wouldn't have gone anywhere. The terrorist attacks of that day shut down all international flights.

I know—the story raises some troubling questions. Why didn't God warn the people aboard the planes that crashed on September 11, 2001? Perhaps he did. God told David not to number the fighting men of Israel; David did anyway and 70,000 men died (1 Chron. 21). There is no searching out the mystery of an event like that. James was martyred; Peter was sprung from jail (Acts 12). We cannot solve the depths of God's work in this world. All we can do is stay very close by his side and listen for his voice, obey his counsel. More depends on it than we know. Those meetings in Scotland and Ireland were remarkable, by the way, and many, many hearts were set free.

PAY ATTENTION TO YOUR HEART

Second, we pay attention to our hearts.

When we set out to hear God's voice, we do not listen as though it will come from somewhere above us or in the room around us. It comes to us from *within,* in the heart, the dwelling place of God. Now, most of us haven't been trained in this, and it's going to take a little practice "tuning in" to all that's going on in there. And there's a lot going on in there, by the way. Many things are trying to play upon the beautiful instrument of the heart. Advertisers are constantly trying to pull on your heartstrings. So is your boss. The devil is a master at manipulating the heart. So are many people— though they would never admit that is what they are doing. How will you know what is compelling you? "Who can map out the various forces at play in one soul?" asked Augustine, a man who was the first to write out the story of listening to his heart. "Man is a great depth, O Lord . . . but the hairs of his head are easier by far to count than . . . the movements of his heart."

This can be distressing at times. All sorts of awful things can seem to issue from your heart—anger, lust, fear, petty jealousies. If you think it's you, a reflection of what's really going on in your heart, it will disable you. It could stop your journey dead in its tracks. What you've encountered is either the voice of your flesh or an attempt of the Enemy to distress you by throwing all sorts of thoughts your way and blaming you for it. You must proceed on this assumption: your heart is good. If it seems that some foul thing is at work there, say to yourself, *Well, then—this is not my heart. My heart is good. I reject this.* Remember Paul in Romans 7? This is not me. *This is not me.* And carry on in your journey. Over time you'll grow familiar with the movements of your heart, and who is trying to influence you there.

We do the same with any counsel or word that presents itself as being from God, but contradicts what he has said to us in his written Word. We walk with wisdom and revelation. When I hear something that seems really unwise, I test it again and again before I launch out. The flesh will try to use your "freedom" to get you to do things you shouldn't do. And now that the Enemy knows you are trying to walk with God and tune in to your heart, he'll play the ventriloquist and try to deceive you there. Any "word" or suggestion that brings discouragement, condemnation, accusation—that is not from God. Neither is confusion, nor any counsel that would lead you to disobey what you do know. Reject it all, and carry on in your journey. Yes, of course, God needs to convict us of sin, warn us of wrong movements in the soul, discipline us for our own good—but the voice of God is never condemning (Rom. 8:1), never harsh or accusing. His conviction brings a desire for repentance; Satan's accusation kills our hearts (2 Cor. 7:10).

Often before I head out on a mission of some sort, I will ask God for his "advance words" to me. It's proven to be a vital part of staying close to him and avoiding disaster. Last fall I was finishing a brutal tour of twenty-eight different trips. As I was heading out for the final engagement—reluctantly, I might add (I asked God to cancel the flight, bring a snowstorm, anything so I didn't have to go)—God said, *Do not give way to cynicism.* I wrote it down in my journal because I forget stuff like this when the forest grows dim and the other voices begin to chatter and chant. But to be honest, I wasn't really sure why he said that.

The trip turned into an ordeal. My flight was delayed; I missed my connection; I missed my ride to the hotel. When I finally got there—around midnight—I hadn't eaten all day. No restaurants were open; I couldn't get to a fast-food joint; the vending machine in the hotel swallowed my last two quarters. The key I was handed led to the last room in the place, overlooking the trash bins. It smelled of thirty years of cigarettes and cheap beer. ("I'm sorry, sir, but the nonsmoking rooms have all been taken. You should have gotten here sooner.") A bare lightbulb hung from the ceiling; the hot water tap didn't work. All sorts of thoughts and impulses began to occur to me: *What a lousy day. Boy, it's great to be in God's service. What a stinking room! This is how this ministry takes care of guests? No wonder nobody wants to come here. I wish I hadn't even come. What a waste of time!* My attitude was going south on a greased pole. Then I remembered God's warning: *Do not give way to cynicism.* Oh. This is what he meant.

I fought cynicism through the hours of the night, battling for my heart. The new day brought a series of beautiful sessions. Rescued again.

STAY CLOSE TO HIS FRIENDS

Third, we get alongside those who walk with God.

I'll say a whole lot more about living in a community that practices the Four Streams later in the book. Put simply, that is what church is supposed to be about. Would that it were. I hope you will find a few folks who walk with God to also walk with you through the seasons of your life. But honesty—and Scripture—forces me to admit they are a rare breed. Few there are who find it. All the more reason for you to make the number less scarce by becoming someone who walks with God and teaches others how.

Look to those who have walked with God down through the ages. Certainly, that is why the Bible is given to us. If God had intended it to be a textbook of doctrine, well, then, he would have written it like one. Oh, yes, we learn many crucial things about doctrine and Christian character in the Scripture, along with a great deal of wisdom. But if you'll flip from cover to cover, you'll notice that it's overwhelmingly a book of stories—tales of men and women who walked with God. Approach the Scriptures not so much as a manual of Christian principles but as the testimony of God's friends on what it means to walk with him through a thousand different episodes. When you are at war, when you are in love, when you have sinned, when you have been given a great gift—this is how you walk with God. Do you see what a different mind-set this is? It's really quite exciting.

And there are those who have walked with God since the canon of Scripture closed. Here is an Athanasius, a Bonaventure, a Julian of Norwich, a Brother Lawrence, an A. W. Tozer—here is how they walked with God. When it comes to time and place, temperament and situation, they could not be more different. Julian lived in a cloister; Tozer lived in Chicago. Athanasius fled to the desert; Lawrence worked in the kitchen. But there is a flavor, a tang, an authenticity to their writings that underlies whatever it is they are trying at the moment to say. Here is someone who knew God, really knew him. This is what it's like to walk with God, and that is what it's like as well.

OTHERWISE . . .

"Most of us are afraid of our guidance, our intuition, our 'hunches,'" warns Agnes Sanford. "We try to close our minds to them, thereby increasing our restlessness and losing the benefit of the heavenly warning that would tell us when and how to pray." My friend Bart is a private pilot. Two weeks ago he flew out to Colorado to take us into a crucial mission of rescuing some of the great warriors of the kingdom. This is the e-mail I received from him afterward:

Had a great flight back to California—a glorious time flying over some of the world's most beautiful country, from the peaks of the San Juans to the depths of the Grand Canyon. But is also very dangerous country to fly over. A loss of flight control would leave few options.

The next day I called maintenance and asked them to take care of a few squawks we identified before I went to Colorado. (The maintenance personnel cleared the safety of the aircraft for this last trip and assured me everything they checked was OK.) As I gave them the airplane to have those items checked again, I asked them something I cannot explain, something I have very seldom thought of and never in the eight years I've owned 17PG have had done. I asked to have the prop balanced. Richard, the manager, said they'd have to send for a specialist to do this, but I said, "Let's have it done."

Yesterday Richard called back. His first words were, "Good call on having the prop balanced. Bart, we found the spinner cracked." (The spinner is the bullet-shaped point in front of the prop.) It is extremely rare for this to occur, and the prop had been replaced just 350 hours ago, which would have yielded this problem at that time. Richard went on to say the points of attachment were cracked almost all the way through the metal, creating a very dangerous situation. If the spinner had detached, it would have been disaster, come right through the windshield. The point of all this is that something or Someone "nudged" me to ask for something to be done on that airplane I have almost never thought of. John, my prayers will be *deliberate* and *often* as I realize how real this battle is going on all around. Thank you for "waking" me to this reality.

Bart

CHAPTER SEVEN

RECEIVING GOD'S INTIMATE COUNSEL

They dress the wound of my people
as though it were not serious.

—GOD (JER. 6:14)

Let us beware of tinkering with our inner life.

—A. W. TOZER

And being very tired and having nothing inside him, he felt so sorry for himself that the tears rolled down his cheeks. What put a stop to all this was a sudden fright. Shasta discovered that someone or somebody was walking beside him. It was pitch dark and he could see nothing. And the Thing (or Person) was going so quietly that he could hardly hear any footfalls. What he could hear was breathing. His invisible companion seemed to breathe on a very large scale . . .

If the horse had been any good—or if he had known how to get any good out of the horse—he would have risked everything on a breakaway and a wild gallop. But he knew he couldn't make that horse gallop. So he went on at a walking pace and the unseen companion walked and breathed beside him. At last he could bear it no longer. "Who are you?" he said, scarcely above a whisper.

"One who has waited long for you to speak," said the Thing. Its voice was not loud, but very large and deep . . .

"Oh please—please do go away. What harm have I ever done you? Oh, I am the unluckiest person in the whole world!" Once more he felt the warm breath of the Thing on his hand and face. "There," it said, "that is not the breath of a ghost. Tell me your sorrows." Shasta was a little reassured by the breath: so he told how he had never known his real father or mother and had been brought up sternly by the fisherman. And then he told the story of his escape and how they were chased by lions and forced to swim for their lives; and of all their dangers in Tashbaan and about his night among the tombs and how the beasts howled at him out of the desert. And he told about the heat and thirst of their desert journey and how they were almost at their goal when another lion chased them and wounded Aravis. And also, how very long it was since he had had anything to eat.

"I do not call you unfortunate," said the Large Voice. "Don't you think it was bad luck to meet so many lions?" said Shasta. "There was only one lion," said the Voice. "What on earth do you mean? I've just told you there were at least two the first night, and . . ." "There was only one; but he was swift of foot." "How do you know?"

"I was the lion."

And as Shasta gaped with open mouth and said nothing, the Voice continued. "I was the lion who forced you to join with Aravis. I was the cat who comforted you among the houses of the dead. I was the lion who drove the jackals from you while you slept. I was the lion who gave the Horses the new strength of fear for the last mile so that you should reach King Lune in time. And I was the lion you do not remember who pushed the boat in which you lay, a child near death, so that it came to shore where a man sat, wakeful at midnight, to receive you."

"Then it was you who wounded Aravis?"

"It was I."

"But what for?"

"Child," said the Voice, "I am telling you your story, not hers."

(C. S. Lewis, *The Horse and His Boy*)

OUR STORY

Our life is a story. A rather long and complicated story that has unfolded over time. There are many scenes, large and small, and many "firsts." Your first step; your first word; your first day of school. There was your first best friend; your first recital; your first date; your first love; your first kiss; your first heartbreak. If you stop and think of it, your heart has lived through quite a story thus far. And over the course of that story your heart has learned many things. Some of what you learned is true; much of it is not. Not when it comes to the core questions about your heart and the heart of God. Is your heart good? Does your heart really matter? What has life taught you about that? Imagine for a moment that God is walking softly beside you. You sense his presence, feel his warm breath. He says, "Tell me your sorrows." What would you say in reply?

"And I will ask the Father, and he will give you another Counselor to be with you forever—the Spirit of truth" (John 14:16–17). Come again? How would you feel if your spouse or a friend said to you, "I think you need some counseling, and so I've arranged for it. You start tomorrow; it'll probably take years"? I've got five bucks that says you'd get more than a little defensive. The combination of our pride—*I don't need any therapy, thank you very much*—and the fact that it's become a *profession*—Freud and Prozac and all that—has kept most of us from realizing that, in fact, we do need counseling. All of us. Jesus sends us his Spirit as Counselor; that ought to make it clear. In fact, we apparently need quite a lot of counsel—the Spirit isn't just stopping in to give us a tune-up; not even an annual checkup. He has come to stay.

Remember, the purpose of this thing called the Christian life is that our hearts might be restored and set free. That's the deal. That's what Jesus came to do, by his own announcement. Jesus wants Life for us, Life with a capital *L*, and that Life comes to us through our hearts. But restoring and releasing the heart is no easy project. God doesn't just throw a switch and poof—it's done. He sends his Counselor to walk with us instead. That tells us it's going to be a *process*. All sorts of damage has been done to your heart over the years, all sorts of terrible things taken in—by sin, by those who should have known better, and by our Enemy, who seeks to steal and kill and destroy the image bearers of God. At best, "hope deferred makes the heart sick" (Prov. 13:12). Certainly, there's been a bit of that in your life. "Even in laughter the heart may ache" (Prov. 14:13), which is to say, things may look fine on the outside, but inside it's another story.

We're told to "trust in the LORD" with all our hearts (Prov. 3:5), but frankly, we find it hard to do. Does trust come easily for you? I would *love* to trust God wholeheartedly. Why is it almost second nature to worry about things? We're told to love one another deeply, "from the heart" (1 Peter 1:22), but that's even more rare. Why is it so easy to get angry at, or to resent, or simply to grow indifferent toward the very people we once loved? The answers lie down in the heart. "For it is with your heart that you believe," Paul says (Rom. 10:10). And in Proverbs we read, "The heart of a man is like deep water, but a man of understanding draws it out" (20:5 NASB). Our deepest convictions—the ones that really shape our lives—they are down there somewhere in the depths of our hearts.

You see, we don't really develop our core convictions so much as they develop within us, when we are young. Down deep, in the inmost parts they form, down in deep water, like the shifting of the continental plates. Certainly, we'd reject the more disabling beliefs if we could; but they form when we are vulnerable, without our really knowing it, like a handprint in wet cement, and over time the cement hardens and there you have it. Think of it this way: Have you always known down deep inside, down to the tips of your toes, that *your* heart is good and that *your* heart matters to God? Me neither. No, what we've come to believe about those ultimate issues was handed to us early on, in most cases by our families.

ASSAULTED FROM OUR YOUTH

Joseph had a dream, and when he told it to his brothers, they hated him all the more. He said to them, "Listen to this dream I had: We were binding sheaves of grain out in the field when suddenly my sheaf rose and stood upright, while your sheaves gathered around mine and bowed down to it." His brothers said to him, "Do you intend to reign over us? Will you actually rule us?" And they hated him all the more because of his dream and what he had said . . .

Now his brothers had gone to graze their father's flocks near Shechem, and Israel said to Joseph, "As you know, your brothers are grazing the flocks near Shechem. Come, I am going to send you to them . . . See if all is well with your brothers and with the flocks, and bring word back to me" . . .

So Joseph went after his brothers and found them near Dothan. But they saw him in the distance, and before he reached them, they plotted to kill him. "Here comes that dreamer!" they said to each other. "Come now, let's kill him and throw him into one of these cisterns and say that a ferocious animal devoured him. Then we'll see what comes of his dreams." (Gen. 37:5–8, 12–14, 17–20)

Joseph stands out, as we were all meant to stand out, each in his or her own way. Instead of celebrating his glory, his brothers want to destroy it. A common story, I'm sorry to say. The worst blows typically come from family. That's where we start our journey of the heart, and that's where we are most vulnerable. What we learned from our parents and siblings about our heart defines us the rest of our days; it becomes the script we live out, for good or for ill. Cinderella's father calls her "a little stunted kitchen wench which my late wife left behind," and her stepmother sees her as "much too dirty, she cannot show herself!" What do you suppose she learned about her heart from growing up in *that* home?

The reason Cinderella's story has stayed with us so many years is that her story is the story of so many little girls. Listen to my friend Abby:

> The assault started as a young girl. There was something about me that seemed to aggravate my father—something about me. Something that seemed to annoy him and repel him. As I grew older, I only seemed to become more frustrating to him. I would ask him a question about how he was doing, and I would watch as the look of annoyance filled his eyes. And I began to suspect that there was something deeply wrong with me, something that made me unlovable, undesirable, something that was "too much" and "not enough," all at once. I tried endlessly to edit my personality, trying to figure out the "right" way to be, the "right" thing to say in every context, in every relationship. And I lived mostly in fear that I was going to "blow" it, and that at any moment the person I loved was going to turn on me, filled with contempt and disdain.

A little girl longs to know that her daddy delights in her, that she is "daddy's girl." What do scenes like this teach a young heart? Abby concluded there was something wrong with her. Most of us believe that, down deep inside. She learned her heart must be bad; certainly, it's not worth fighting for. And God? Well, her heart mustn't really matter to him, either. After all, he let it happen. He didn't intervene.

Even after receiving Jesus into my heart, this suspicion of something "dark and wrong" haunted me. I began to find myself especially anxious around animals and children, certain that in their piercing intuition they would sense this darkness in me and my vain attempts to cover it up. And I would be exposed. One time, while horseback riding, my horse knocked me against the limb of the tree. The limb ripped me off my saddle and I tumbled down onto the ground. My eyes filled with hot tears and my heart with waves of self-contempt. The voice within me said, *See, there really is something dark about you. That horse sensed it and he just wanted to get you off of him, whatever it took.*

There is David, whose heart of glory rises like the sun, full of faith and courage when he sees that no one will take on Goliath. Though he is only a youth, untrained for war, he is outraged that an "uncircumcised Philistine" has dared to taunt the armies of the living God. He announces, "Let no one lose heart on account of this Philistine; your servant will go and fight him" (1 Sam. 17:32). David's oldest brother was among the soldiers of Israel who *should* have had the heart to face Goliath but rehearsed his excuses instead. His cowardice is exposed by David's bravery after he lashes out: "Why have you come down here? And with whom did you leave those few sheep in the desert? I know how conceited you are and how wicked your heart is; you came down only to watch the battle" (1 Sam. 17:28). Ah, family.

The worst blows tend to come from those who know us well and should have loved us. In the German myth, Siegfried was a great warrior; he slew a terrible dragon; he was fearless in battle. Siegfried was invincible—except for a small place on his back, between his shoulders. There, he could be wounded. An uncle discovered Siegfried's "weak spot" and murdered him. Stabbed in the back. By family. Small wonder this tale has endured through time.

MISUNDERSTOOD

Even Jesus endured this sort of assault—not the open accusation that he had a wicked heart, but the more subtle kind, the seemingly "innocent" arrows that come through "misunderstanding."

> After this, Jesus went around in Galilee, purposely staying away from Judea because the Jews there were waiting to take his life. But when the Jewish Feast of Tabernacles was near, Jesus' brothers said to him, "You ought to leave here and go to Judea, so that your disciples may see the miracles you do. No one who wants to become a public figure acts in secret. Since you are doing these things, show yourself to the world." For even his own brothers did not believe in him. (John 7:1–5)

I think we can relate to that. Did your family believe in you? Some did—but far too many more believe in the person *they* wanted you to be. Did they even notice your heart at all? Have they been thrilled in your choices, or has their disappointment made it clear that you just aren't what you're supposed to be? At another point in his ministry, Jesus' family shows up to collect him. "Your mother and brothers are standing outside, wanting to see you" (Luke 8:20). They think he's lost it, and they've come to bring him home, poor man. Misunderstanding is damaging, more insidious because we don't identify it as an attack on the heart. How subtly it comes, sowing doubt and discouragement where there should have been validation and support. There must be something wrong with us.

I'm not big on computer games personally. But my eldest son, Sam, is an absolute crackerjack at them. It's a point of tension in our relationship. I don't think he ought to spend so much time there, and he thinks he's not given enough. Though I try to hide my distaste because I know how much he loves playing Off Road Fury and Delta Force, it's pretty obvious when I never play with him. Just yesterday Sam said to me, "You and Mom don't like computer games, so I feel like you don't like me." Ouch. I missed a part of his glory, shamed a part of his heart. How many an artist has been crushed in a family that prefers a "rational" approach to life? How many an engineer dismissed by a family of musicians? How many of us are lost in life simply because no one in our early world saw our glory and affirmed it?

"How long, O men, will you turn my glory into shame?" (Ps. 4:2). These blows aren't random or incidental. They strike directly at some part of the heart, turn the very thing God created to be a source of celebration into a source of shame. And so you can at least begin to discover your glory by looking more closely at what you were shamed for. Look at what's been assaulted, used, abused. As Bernard of Clairvaux declared, "Through the heart's wound, I see its secret."

Let me put it this way: What has life taught you about your God-given glory? What have you believed about your heart over the years? "That it's not worth anyone's time," said a woman. Her parents were too busy to really want to know her. "That it's weak," confided a friend. He suffered several emasculating blows as a boy, and his father simply shamed him for it. "That I shouldn't trust it to anyone." "That it's selfish and self-centered." "That it's bad." And you . . . what have you believed?

Those accusations you heard growing up, those core convictions that formed about your heart, will remain down there until someone comes to dislodge them, run them out of Dodge.

THE WONDERFUL COUNSELOR

None of this was your fault.

I was visiting my parents a year ago last summer, and as you well know, that has a way of stirring the pot, bringing all sorts of debris to the surface. For many people, family is like kryptonite. You remember, the one substance that zapped Superman's strength. It seems that no matter how much we've grown, how long we've been away, how far we've traveled in our own journeys, when we go back to family, we are suddenly children again. All the old dynamics, the patterns, the messages—they're all back, trying to pull us down. So you'll understand when I made up some excuse about running to the market for a few things. I simply had to get out of the house, take a drive. I needed some air.

I drove to the neighborhood of an old girlfriend, my first girl-friend, who years upon years ago broke my heart. The first cut is the deepest, as the saying goes. It wasn't simply what happened with her that I wanted to remember; our breakup happened at the time in my life when everything else was coming down around me like a house of cards. My father's alcoholism. The collapse of my family. When it rains, it pours. I thought I had found in my first love a refuge from all that. And I did . . . for a time. Then she sent me away, for no reason I could find out. All the arrows landed in the same place in my heart: you don't matter; you're not worth fighting for; there's something wrong with you.

For years now I've lived with the fear that at some point, everyone is going to leave, and I will be left alone. For no reason I can say, in no way I can prevent, I am going to wind up alone. I can't really explain why, but I know it's my fault. It lingers there, down under the surface, like a chronic backache or a low-grade fever. But it colors everything I say and do; it shapes every relationship. I remain guarded, distant. I feel I ought to do more, be more. So it becomes a self-fulfilling prophecy. And I'm sick of it.

I parked the car and simply let the tears come, allowed the memories to take me to the place in my heart that was pierced by the loss of those I loved, "loved but did not understand in my youth," as Norman MacLean said. Somehow, being in the old neighborhoods again, smelling all the old familiar smells, hearing the voices of the past, brought this unhealed place to the surface. And Jesus walked softly beside.

None of this was your fault.

Now, you must understand, I didn't know that for all those years I had believed it *was* my fault. I didn't think about it much at all. But down in the deep waters of my soul that conviction had settled, grown, like barnacles on a shipwreck, lies clinging to my heart. *This all happened because my heart is bad; it's my fault.* And down the Spirit went to speak the words to break those lies. *None of this was your fault.* And something of my heart came free that night.

> I'm standing before my old high school.
> It's been ten years since I touched the door.
> But to heal the old pain we must face it again
> so I'll walk down that hallway once more.
> I have come to this ten year reunion
> for my heart is still prisoner of war.
> That's what I came back here for. (David Wilcox, "Last Chance Waltz")

ASK GOD

Peter was one of Jesus' closest friends, one of only three invited into his innermost circle. Christ brought him up to the Mount of

Transfiguration to see his glory unveiled. Only two others got to see this (James and John); the rest of the gang waited at the base. They waited outside the door as well, when Christ went in to raise Jairus's daughter from the dead. But Peter got to come in with him. In Gethsemane, at his hour of greatest need, Jesus again took Peter aside, poured his heart out to him; he looked to Peter for strength. Three years of this, and who knows how many other stories. Peter must have known, *I have a special place in Jesus' heart.* So, how do you suppose Peter felt after he denied Christ—not just once, but three times? It must have been devastating.

After the Resurrection, Jesus is on the beach with Peter and the others. It's a touching reunion. Following a night of lousy fishing, Christ yells out to the guys to let their nets down for a catch—just as he did that morning he first called them. Again, their nets are bursting with the load. Just like the good old days. Peter leaps from the boat and swims to Christ. They have breakfast together. Reunited, laughing about the catch, relaxed, warmed by the fire, and stuffed from breakfast, Jesus then turns to Peter.

> When they had finished eating, Jesus said to Simon Peter, "Simon son of John, do you truly love me more than these?" "Yes, Lord," he said, "you know that I love you." Jesus said, "Feed my lambs." Again Jesus said, "Simon son of John, do you truly love me?" He answered, "Yes, Lord, you know that I love you." Jesus said, "Take care of my sheep." The third time he said to him, "Simon son of John, do you love me?" Peter was hurt because Jesus asked him the third time, "Do you love me?" He said, "Lord, you know all things; you know that I love you." Jesus said, "Feed my sheep." (John 21:15–17)

What a beautiful story. Notice first that Christ does not let Peter sweep the whole matter under the rug. If this issue isn't addressed, it will haunt the old fisherman for the rest of his life. A nagging guilt will make it hard to pray. That sense of *Who are you kidding?* will be there every time Peter tries to tell others about Jesus. No, this must be spoken to. Most of us simply try to "put things behind us," get past it, forget the pain as quickly as we can. Really—denial is a favorite method of coping for many Christians. But not with Jesus. He wants truth in the inmost being, and to get it there he's got to *take us into* our inmost being. One way he'll do this is by bringing up an old memory. You'll be driving down the road and suddenly remember something from your childhood. Or maybe you'll have a dream about a long-forgotten person, event, or place. However he brings it up, go with him there. He has something to say to you.

Notice also that Jesus asks Peter the penetrating question three times—once for every betrayal. Peter is hurt by it, and that is the point. The lessons that have been laid down in pain can be accessed only in pain. Christ must open the wound, not just bandage it over. Sometimes he'll take us there by having an event repeat itself years later, only with new characters in the current situation. We find ourselves overlooked for a job, just as we were overlooked by our parents. Or we experience fear again, just as we felt those lonely nights in our room upstairs. These are all *invitations* to go with him into the deep waters of the heart, uncover the lies buried down there, and bring in the truth that will set us free. Don't just bury it quickly; ask God what he is wanting to speak to.

There are two things we need to know, maybe above all else. We need to know that our heart is good, and that our heart matters to God. I've found that for most folks, this is what's been most assaulted; this is what we most doubt. We can't just talk ourselves into this; Jesus must show us. He must take us there, as he did with Peter. So ask him. Ask God to show you that your heart is good, and that you do matter to him. I recently received this e-mail from a young woman who took my advice:

On Monday, I ventured over to the park for just some time in beauty. The sun was slowly making its way down, and as I watched, my heart just ached to receive what God was whispering: "Karen, yes your heart is good, ever since you let me come in and dwell there . . . but." And I stopped there. It was getting dark, and I had things to do. So I made my way back to my car . . . slowly. A few steps later, I heard God say that He wouldn't let me leave without hearing the rest of it. But I kept walking, until I just couldn't go any further—dang it. I knew that He wanted to be with me in a place that was not comfortable, was not "safe," not in my car where no one could see me. Oh no . . . it had to be there in a public wilderness. For that was part of the freedom that my heart needed—release from trying to "save" face and release from caring so much what people think of me (the lies that killed my heart as a leader in the church).

The tears of grief flowed freely down my face. He began to show me and I let Him. I was reminded of all of the recurring assaults, and with each arrow He spoke to me His shield, "You see, Karen, that lie? That was the assault to keep you from connecting. That lie? That one was to make you fearful and anxious. That brutal arrow? That was to keep you from glorifying ME. Ah . . . but Karen, in the places where those lies targeted . . . your heart was good. It is good." As God spoke, I wept. I've so needed to grieve where my heart has been lost. I've needed to find it! I got mad at the lies and strategies that Satan has used on me. Wow. Little did I know that a huge part of the freedom God has been aching for me to experience would come from asking our Abba to "show me that my heart is good."

I have a number of stories like that as well; they are beautiful and precious to me. It might be one of the hardest and richest things you ever do. Ask God to reveal to you that the new covenant is true. Your heart is good. And your heart matters. Deeply.

THE HELP OF OTHERS

Now I was indeed in a pitiful plight. There was literally nothing in the tower but my shadow and me. The walls rose right up to the roof; in which, as I had seen from without, there was one little square opening. This I now knew to be the only window the tower possessed. I sat down on the floor, in listless wretchedness.

More earnestly than ever, I longed for freedom; more drearily than ever, crept on the next wretched day. I measured by the sunbeams, caught through the little window in the trap of my tower, how it went by, waiting only for the dreams of night.

About noon, I started as if something foreign to all my senses and all my experience had suddenly invaded me; yet it was only the voice of a woman singing. My whole frame quivered with joy, surprise, and the sensation of the unforeseen. Like a living soul, like an incarnation of Nature, the song entered my prison-house. Each tone folded its wings, and laid itself, like a caressing bird, upon my heart. It bathed me like a sea; enrapt me like an odorous vapor; entered my soul like a long draught of clear spring water; shone upon me like essential sunlight; soothed me like a mother's voice and hand.

Hardly knowing what I did, I opened the door. Why had I not done so before? I do not know. At first I could see no one; but when I forced myself past the tree which grew across the entrance, I saw, seated on the ground and leaning against the tree, with her back to my prison, a beautiful woman. She looked up at me and smiled. "Ah! Were you the prisoner there? I am very glad I have wiled you out." (George MacDonald, *Phantastes*)

I want to be careful, lest I have painted a wrong picture here. This stream of Counseling doesn't just flow to us directly from Christ, *only* from him. It flows through his people as well. We need others—and need them deeply. Yes, the Spirit was sent to be our Counselor. Yes, Jesus speaks to us personally. But often he works through another human being. The fact is, we are usually too close to our lives to see what's going on. Because it's *our* story we're trying to understand, we sometimes don't know what's true or false, what's real and imagined. We can't see the forest for the trees. It often takes the eyes of someone to whom we can tell our story, bare our souls. The more dire our straits, the more difficult it can be to hear directly from God.

In every great story the hero or heroine must turn to someone older or wiser for the answer to some riddle. Dorothy seeks the Wizard; Frodo turns to Gandalf; Neo has Morpheus; and Curdie is helped by the Lady of the Silver Moon. Several years ago there was a woman who wiled me out of my prison, a prison of my own making. It was in my final year of graduate studies for a degree in counseling. Naturally, I thought by this time I pretty much had it all together. Why, I was about to become a professional counselor. Danger sign number one. Pride is so blinding. Her name was Joy, and she was . . . eventually. But first she had to cut through my facade.

As a part of our course requirement, we had to meet with a graduate assistant for an hour each week. This being a Christian program, I thought she would go after my sin. Instead, she went after my glory. No one had ever done that before.

"Why are you holding back?" she asked.

I hesitated, stalled. "I'm not sure what you're talking about."

"Yes, you do. You are holding back, playing it safe."

I was squirming. Is this what Adam felt as he heard the voice of God coming closer to his hiding place in the bushes? *Where are you?*

"Now, you're gifted enough to pull it off, make it *look* like you're engaged with us. But you are running on only six cylinders; I know you have eight. Come forward and lead us."

It was more than a little unnerving. I'd been seen; I'd been found out. But not as a disappointment, not as a bad heart exposed. Rather, it was my glory that had been seen, and it was being asked for. What do you do with *that*?

Over the course of several months my whole system of perfectionism-so-as-not-to-be-seen unraveled. *Maybe* . . . the thought began to creep in . . . *maybe the world has been wrong about me.* "The world has been wrong about you. They've hated your glory—just as the Evil One hates the glory of God. But we need your gift. Come forth." I began to believe the truth, and it set me free. The doctrine I knew—kind of. But having a doctrine pass before the mind is not what the Bible means by knowing the truth. It's only when it reaches down deep into the heart that the truth begins to set us free, just as a key must penetrate a lock to turn it, or as rainfall must saturate the earth down to the roots in order for your garden to grow.

Listen to the rest of Abby's story:

God has given me a new name, a name that is so perfectly and wondrously opposite of the lie that had controlled so much of my life. And he is healing my heart. A year ago, a wise woman whom I deeply respect was praying for me. She heard God call me "My Sunshine and my delight." *Really . . . really?* My heart responded. *Sunshine? Not darkness? Not object of my contempt?* This was so precious to me, so beyond my wildest hopes for who I was to my God, that I kept it to myself. Over the next several months, two friends wrote to me completely independent of one another, and in their letters they both described that I was like "sunshine" in their lives. Still, I kept this in my heart. Then, my boss and dear friend began to call me "Sunshine." I could barely believe it! And finally, a dear friend saw a painting of a young girl and instantly "recognized" my face in it. The young girl had a look of confidence and mischief, and utter security in who she was and to whom she belonged. The name of the painting was "Jessica of the Sunlight Ranch."

God was calling to me—God was calling to me to believe that truly I was "his sunshine and his delight." Calling me to believe that there was something beautiful and valiant that he had placed deep within me that my husband, my friends, that this world needs. Calling me to believe that the effect of my life is "goodness and light and *life*"; not darkness and contempt and irritation. And so I've started offering my heart. I've started saying no to the voice of my enemy that calls me to fearfully tone down, edit, control my words and my actions for fear of "offending" or bringing on rejection and shame. Instead, I've been stepping out. I've been sharing what I see of my God and in my friends. I've chosen to offer my presence, my heart, and my love, instead of trying endlessly to figure out what else I should offer. I've chosen to believe I am loved and safe with my God.

"Behold, You desire truth in the innermost being" (Ps. 51:6 NASB). Getting it there is the work of the stream we'll call Counseling—Receiving God's Intimate Counsel.

CHAPTER EIGHT

DEEP RESTORATION

He heals the brokenhearted
  and binds up their wounds.

—PSALM 147:3

Look at me—I'm shattered.

—THE ROLLING STONES

For at that moment a curious little procession was approaching—eleven Mice, six of whom carried between them something on a litter made of branches, but the litter was no bigger than a large atlas. No one has ever seen mice more woebegone than these. They were plastered with mud—some with blood too—and their ears were down and their whiskers drooped and their tails dragged in the grass, and their leader piped on his slender pipe a melancholy tune. On the litter lay what seemed little better than a damp heap of fur; all that was left of Reepicheep. He was still breathing, but more dead than alive, gashed with innumerable wounds, one paw crushed, and, where his tail had been, a bandaged stump.

"Now, Lucy," said Aslan.

Lucy had her diamond bottle out in a moment. Though only a drop was needed on each of Reepicheep's wounds, the wounds were so many that there was a long and anxious silence before she had finished and the Master Mouse sprang from the litter. His hand went at once to his sword hilt, with the other he twirled his whiskers. He bowed.

"Hail, Aslan!" (C. S. Lewis, *Prince Caspian*)

A House Divided

Yes, we have all been wounded in this battle. And we will be wounded again. But something deeper has happened to us than mere wounds.

I expect that all of us at one time or another have said, "Well, part of me wants to, and another part of me doesn't." You know the feeling—part of you pulled one direction, part of you the other. Part of me loves writing and genuinely looks forward to a day at my desk. But not all of me. Sometimes I'm also afraid of it. Part of me fears that I will fail—that I am simply stating what is painfully obvious, or saying something vital but incoherent. I'm drawn to it, and I also feel ambivalent about it. Come to think of it, I feel that way about a lot of things. Part of me wants to go ahead and dive into friendship, take the risk. I'm tired of living alone. Another part says, *Stay away—you'll get hurt. Nobody really cares anyway.* Part of me says, *Wow! Maybe God really is going to come through for me.* Another voice rises up and says, *You are on your own.*

Don't you sometimes feel like a house divided?

Take your little phobias. Why are you afraid of heights or intimacy or public speaking? All the discipline in the world wouldn't get you to go skydiving, share something really personal in a small group, or take the pulpit next Sunday. Why do you hate it when people touch you or criticize you? And what about those little "idiosyncrasies" you can't give up to save your life? Why do you bite your nails? Why do you work so many hours? Why do you get irritated at these questions? You won't go out unless your makeup is perfect—why is that? Other women don't mind being seen in their grubbies. Something in you "freezes" when your dad calls—what's that all about? You clean and organize; you demand perfection—did you ever wonder *why*?

I think we've just assumed all that stuff is our battle with "the flesh." And yes, there is a civil war waged between the new heart and the old nature. Romans 7–8 describes it quite well. Part of me doesn't want to love my neighbor—not when his son just backed his car into my Jeep and smashed it up. I want to take the little brat to court. Part of me knows that prayer is essential; another part of me would rather turn on the TV and check out. And that whole bit about being long-suffering—no way. Part of me wants to just get drunk. And that is the part I must crucify daily, give no ground to, make no alliance with. It's not the true me (Rom. 7:22). It's my battle with the flesh. We all know that battle well. But that is not what I'm wanting to explore here.

No, there's something else we are describing when we say, "Well, part of me wants to and part of me doesn't." It's more than a figure of speech. We might not know it, but something really significant is being revealed in those remarks. There are these places that we cannot seem to get beyond. Everything is going along just fine, and then—boom. Something suddenly brings you to tears or makes you furious, depressed, or anxious, and you cannot say why. I'll tell you why.

We are not wholehearted.

BROKENHEARTED

A few years ago a woman pulled me aside to tell me that her marriage was in trouble. Her husband, a kind and patient man, had simply reached his limit with her obsessive-compulsive behavior. Their home was being overrun by puppies—not the live version, but the stuffed little critters. She collected them ravenously, hundreds of doggies, large and small. In fact, she snatched up *anything* that had a puppy on it—plates, pictures, pillows, posters. For several years she was able to contain it to her bedroom, but it had eventually overrun the entire house. Now, I think a stuffed dog or two are probably good things to have around, but having more than a hundred does raise some concerns. Anytime we find ourselves doing something we wish we could stop but cannot, it ought to raise some concerns. For that matter, anytime we find ourselves *unable* to do the very thing we want to do, it also ought to raise some concerns.

She told me that when she was a very young girl of four or five, she had a little toy puppy that was her playmate. You know how that goes—they went everywhere together. The two of them had tea parties. He went to kindergarten in her backpack. He took all the family trips with her. This little puppy—Scruffy was his name—had the place of honor in her bedroom, upon her pillow every night. He was her special friend. That is, until the day her father in a fit of rage ripped the head off Scruffy while she stood crying before him, begging her daddy not to hurt him. It was the kind of blow that shatters a little girl's heart. It's not just about a stuffed animal, of course. The assault brought terror into her relationship with her daddy, cast a shadow over her whole young world, shattered all security. Fifty-some years later, she is unable to make herself stop collecting puppies, and she cannot tell you why.

When Isaiah promised that the Messiah will come to heal the brokenhearted, he was not speaking poetically. The Bible does use metaphor, as in when Jesus says, "I am the gate" (John 10:9). Of course, he is not an *actual* gate like the kind you slammed yesterday; he has no hinges on his body, no knob you turn. He is using metaphor. But when Isaiah talks about the brokenhearted, God is not using metaphor. The Hebrew is *leb shabar* (*leb* for "heart," *shabar* for "broken"). Isaiah uses the word *shabar* to describe a bush whose "twigs are dry, they are broken off" (27:11); to describe the idols of Babylon lying "shattered on the ground" (21:9), as a statue shatters into a thousand pieces when you knock it off the table; or to describe a broken bone (38:13). God is speaking literally here. He says, "Your heart is now in many pieces. I want to heal it."

The heart can be broken—literally. Just like a branch or a statue or a bone. Can you name any precious thing that *can't*? Certainly, we've seen that the mind can be broken—or what are all those mental institutions for? Most of the wandering, muttering "homeless" people pushing a shopping cart along have a broken mind. The will can be broken too. Have you seen photos of concentration camp prisoners? Their eyes are cast down; something in them is defeated. They will do whatever they are told. But somehow we have overlooked the fact that this treasure called the heart can also be broken, *has* been broken, and now lies in pieces down under the surface. When it comes to "habits" we cannot quit or patterns we cannot stop, anger that flies out of nowhere, fears we cannot overcome or weaknesses we hate to admit—much of what troubles us comes out of the broken places in our hearts crying out for relief.

In the case of the woman obsessed with puppies, part of her heart was broken when she was five, and that part of her *remains* young and afraid and desperate for someone to come and protect her, restore her puppy to her. Those aren't the actions of a fifty-something woman; they are the cries of a five-year-old heart. Surely, there are things you do that you cannot provide a reasonable explanation for. Those of you unable to resist a jelly donut—certainly, that is a hunger for more than sweets. Love, perhaps? Comfort? The drive that keeps you late at the office—what is it you are hoping for? Approval? For someone to finally say, "We're so very proud of you"?

I know losing a toy puppy seems rather innocuous, given the horrifying things done to some children. And some of you are thinking, *I wish all I was doing was collecting puppies,* given the dark and dangerous things some people find themselves doing. The mother who passes out in front of her children for love of alcohol. The young man dying of AIDS for the love he's been seeking with other men. But there is something common in all these stories. Something inside is compelling them to do things they do not want to do. What that usually indicates is a broken heart. Those actions are attempts to nurse or repair a rift in the soul.

A fine young man I know is absolutely beside himself with anxiety whenever he begins to care deeply for another person. Now, this is not a man given over to fits of weeping. He is for the most part a fine, upstanding Christian man. But when he draws near to love, this tough construction worker starts to shake all over and cry uncontrollably for reasons he cannot explain. When he was young, his father walked out on him and his mom. It was, as it should have been, devastating. Later on, a girlfriend did the exact same thing to him. Now, he's prayed lots about this; he's had some counseling; he's memorized lots of Scripture on the faithfulness of God and all that. It hasn't changed things. He's still absolutely undone at the approach of possible abandonment. It's like an earthquake in the soul. There's some rift or fault line down there.

Yet another indication of a house divided is the "on again, off again" personality. One day you are kind; the next day you are sullen and angry. One day you are inspired by Christ, captured for his purposes; the next day, you are completely driven by the world. Sure—we all have bad days. Lord knows, PMS and traffic jams can bring on some dramatic changes. But I'm talking about a pattern that is repeated again and again.

I know a man just like that; he's so hard to read, you never know what you're going to get. He'll be completely committed to following Christ one moment, and the next he's watching his stocks and totally absorbed in his businesses. It's not bad to keep an eye on things; but being so totally absorbed to the point that everything else—*everyone* else—suffers, that's not so good. It's like somebody threw a switch inside him. Not a Dr. Jekyll–Mr. Hyde, just a man so completely different depending on what part of his heart he's living out of. He is not wholehearted.

It doesn't take a major assault like sexual abuse to create a broken heart, by the way. This is so important to understand, for many good people assume they haven't any real brokenness because they haven't endured the horrors they read about in the paper or watch on TV. Depending on the age or circumstances, it can be an embarrassing moment like stuttering in front of the class or hearing a harsh word from your mother. The bottom line is, Jesus speaks as though we are all the brokenhearted. We would do well to trust his perspective on this.

THE STREAM OF HEALING OR DEEP RESTORATION

For this people's heart has become calloused;
    they hardly hear with their ears,
    and they have closed their eyes.
Otherwise they might see with their eyes,
    hear with their ears,
    understand with their hearts
and turn, and I would heal them. (Matt. 13:15)

"And I would heal them." That's a different offer from: "And I would forgive them." It's a different offer from: "And I will give them a place in heaven." No, Jesus is offering *healing* to us. Look at what he does to people who are broken. How does he handle them? The blind are able to see like a hawk. The deaf are able to hear a pin drop. The lame do hurdles. The corroding skin of the leper is cleansed and made new. The woman with the issue of blood stops hemorrhaging. The paralyzed servant hops out of bed. They are, every last one of them, healed. Now follow this closely: everything Jesus *did* was to illustrate what he was trying to *say*. Here—look at this—this is what I'm offering to do for you. Not just for your body, but more important, for your soul. I can heal your heart. I can restore your soul.

> The LORD is my shepherd, I shall not be in want.
>> He makes me lie down in green pastures,
> he leads me beside quiet waters,
>> he restores my soul. (Ps. 23:1–3)

> He heals the brokenhearted
>> and binds up their wounds. (Ps. 147:3)

> Heal me, O LORD, and I will be healed;
>> save me and I will be saved,
>> for you are the one I praise. (Jer. 17:14)

> For you who revere my name, the sun of righteousness will rise with healing in its wings. (Mal. 4:2)

> He welcomed them and spoke to them about the kingdom of God, and healed those who needed healing. (Luke 9:11)

For some reason, this has been lost in much of the recent offerings of Christianity. Perhaps it has been our pride, which has kept us from admitting that we are broken. Lord knows, I've done that for years—probably am still doing it now. Perhaps it is our fear of getting our hopes up; it seems too good to be true. Perhaps it's been the almost total focus on sin and the Cross. But the Scripture is abundant and clear: Christ came not only to pardon us, but also to heal us. He wants the glory restored. So, put the book down for just a moment, and let this sink in: Jesus can, and wants to, heal your heart. What does that rouse in you? Is it hope? Is it cynicism? Is it "I tried that—it doesn't work"?

It was only a few months ago that I woke in the wee hours of the morning to fear . . . again. How many other times had I simply jumped into my day as fast as I could—shower, shave, rush off to work—hounded by a nameless fear, trying to bury it with a heap of busyness? I thought somehow that if I just ran hard enough, it wouldn't catch up to me. Perfectionism was my refuge. But this morning, thank God, was different. I'm tired of running, like the prodigal, I suppose. Sooner or later you're just going to have to turn and face things. I lay there in bed and let the fear rise up, let it come. And as it came, I began to ask a question of both myself and God: *What am I afraid of?* The sense I had was that *I'm going to blow it—badly. I'm about to make a mess of things.* Now, there was nothing in my life at the time on the brink of falling apart. Things were going well. But staying with it, I invited Christ to come into the fear and speak to me there. *Jesus, what is this all about?*

When have you felt like this before?

Two memories came to me. The feeling of *I'm blowing it badly* took me there. The first was the day I got arrested for "breaking and entering," police jargon for robbing a house. I was fifteen years old at the time, spinning out of control, my family falling apart at home. It was a deeply shameful experience, and no one talked to me about it; no one showed me the way out. The second memory came quickly on the heels of the first, as if it had to come now or I'd never let it: the day my girlfriend got an abortion. It might be the most horrifying day of my life. I don't think we really knew what we were doing, but somewhere deeper in my soul I knew whatever was happening, it was really, really bad. That one was so dark I just buried it deep and never, ever spoke of it again.

As each event came back to me, all I could do was invite Jesus in. *Yes, Lord, thank you for bringing this back. Come in and meet me here; speak to me here.* I asked his forgiveness for my part in the burglary and in the abortion. I asked him to come and heal those wounds and bring what was true about my heart *to* my heart. And he did; he counseled me deeply. But that wasn't the end of it. Several weeks later the fear came back. A month after that it came again. There was something broken in me, something that allowed the fear to keep returning, no matter how many comforting things Christ said. I needed a different stream.

A PERSONAL HEALING

A remarkable and unlooked-for healing came to me the same day I nearly killed myself in the Collegiate Peaks Wilderness in Colorado. It was early summer, when the melting snows began to give us back the high country, and I had gone into the wilderness on a four-day backpacking trip. I went alone—well, that is to say, I went without another human companion. Scout, my golden retriever, came along, much to his boundless joy. It had been a very emotionally and spiritually intense spring, and I desperately needed to find my heart and God again. (The two go hand in hand, of course. Without your heart you cannot hope to find God, for the heart is his dwelling place. If you ignore your heart, it's like looking for him everywhere but at home.)

On the third day I tried to cross a ridge between two valleys. No trail existed there, but I thought from the map that it could be done, and I'd even talked to a ranger at the trailhead on my first day who told me he'd heard of people crossing that pass. I began to negotiate my way down the far side of the ridge on what seemed to be an ancient game trail, but after about one hundred feet the ground beneath me disappeared; below me a cliff simply dropped straight down for more than seven hundred feet. I was forced to backtrack, climbing my way back to the top of the pass with a sixty-pound pack and a very reluctant retriever. It became so dangerous I was forced to leave Scout on a ledge, climb to the top to dump my pack, and make a second trip down for the dog. Hours later we slumped back into the very camp we'd broken that morning—tails dragging, exhausted, frightened, confused.

The air grew chill as the sun began to set, so I went and sat on a rock in the last rays to get warm. Tears began to flow, though I could not have told you why. I sensed the presence of Jesus with me, felt he was speaking to some young and frightened place in my heart. At first the movements of God in me were inarticulate, deeper than words. Then, slowly, I began to tune in to what seemed like a conversation between Jesus and a sort of young place in my soul. It was as if I was eavesdropping; Jesus had just asked a question, and my heart—it felt like the heart of a very young boy—replied, *He's always doing that to me.* Oops. I knew the "he" in question was me, and "that" was what happened up on the ridge. I felt like an older brother caught making his younger brother jump off the roof.

Will you let me heal you?

I wasn't sure whether the question was for the "young" me or the "old" me, so I waited and listened in humbled silence. Jesus was speaking to the young and frightened place in my heart. (How many years have I lived in fear? Far too many.) This is what he nearly always does when he comes to mend those rifts in our hearts.

He brings his comfort and mercy to those times and places where we suffered the shattering blow, and the heart in that place often feels the same age as it was at the time of the event, even though it might have been decades ago. More tears.

It might be a surprise that Christ asks our permission to come in and heal, but you may remember that famous passage from Revelation, "Behold, I stand at the door and knock" (3:20 NKJV). He doesn't force his way in, and the principle remains true after we have given Christ the initial access to our hearts that we call salvation. There are rooms we have kept locked up, places he has not had access to by our own will, and in order to experience his healing, we must also give him permission to come in there. *Will you let me heal you?* Something in me . . . hesitated. *Only if he'll stop doing that to me.*

Then it was as if the gaze of Christ had turned to me—the "older" me—and what he said was, *It's true, John. You know you are very hard on your heart. You are not merciful with those broken places within you.* He's right, of course—I'm not. They are a nuisance. I don't like feeling as though there is a young and fearful boy inside, and I handle that by shoving those fears down and pushing myself on. I think that's how most of us handle the young and broken places within; we simply try to get past them, push them down, hide them as much as possible, and get on with life. Thank God, Jesus is much more compassionate. I felt I needed to repent of my drivenness, and after a prayer to that effect, I sensed the young part give Christ permission to come in.

The work of Christ in healing the soul is a deep mystery, more amazing than open-heart surgery. A friend described his experience as having Christ "holding the broken parts of my heart in his hands, and bringing them all together, holding them tenderly until his life brought a wholeness or a oneness to what was many pieces." Yes— that's it. That idea of "binding up" our brokenness involves bring- ing all the shattered pieces back together into one whole heart.

Reintegrating those places broken off by tragedy or assault. It was as if Jesus took this broken part of me and loved me there, brought me into the safety of his presence, brought this part "home."

The sun set. All was quiet. I felt . . . lighter. Gladder. The fear was gone. In its place came a great surprise—joy. Something had been healed, restored, mended. I went around the woods gathering firewood while singing a sort of make-it-up-as-you-go kind of song a young boy would sing when he was happy. It was but one event in an amazing journey that began several years ago when I prayed this simple but earnest prayer: *Jesus, I want my whole heart back.*

TOWARD RESTORATION

> We simply invoke His Presence, then invite Him into our hearts. He shows us our hearts. In prayer for the healing of memories, we simply ask our Lord to come present to that place where we were so wounded (or perhaps wounded another). Forgiving others, and receiving forgiveness, occurs. In prayer for the healing of the heart from fears, bitterness, etc., we see primal fears as well as lesser ones dealt with immediately: those fears that the sufferer often has not been aware of, never been able to name—they only know that their lives have been seriously restricted and shaped because of them. (Leanne Payne, *The Healing Presence*)

Walking with God leads to receiving his intimate counsel, and counseling leads to deep restoration. As we learn to walk with God and hear his voice, he is able to bring up issues in our hearts that need speaking to. Some of those wounds were enough to break our hearts, create a rift in the soul, and so we need his healing as well. This is something Jesus walks us into—sometimes through the help of another person who can listen and pray with us, sometimes with God alone. As David said in Psalm 23, he leads us away, to a quiet place, to restore the soul. Our first choice is to go with him there—to slow down, unplug, accept the invitation to come aside. You won't find healing in the midst of the Matrix. We need time in the presence of God. This often comes on the heels of God's raising some issue in our hearts or after we've just relived an event that takes us straight to that broken place, or waking as I did to a raw emotion.

> Teach me your way, O LORD,
>> and I will walk in your truth;
> give me an undivided heart,
>> that I may fear your name.
> I will praise you, O Lord my God, with all my heart;
>> I will glorify your name forever. (Ps. 86:11–12)

When we are in the presence of God, removed from distractions, we are able to hear him more clearly, and a secure environment has been established for the young and broken places in our hearts to surface. We ask God to surround us with his presence. We give ourselves back over to him, come under his authority, for as Paul warns, it is possible to lose connection with our Head, who is Christ (Col. 2:19). We declare the authority of Jesus over our hearts, for he made our hearts (Ps. 33:15) and he has redeemed our hearts (Rom. 2:29).

> *Jesus, I come into your presence now, and I ask you to surround me. I come under your authority and your claim upon my life. I give myself to you—body, soul, and spirit. I give my heart to you, in every way—including the broken places in me. I declare your authority over my heart, for you made my heart and you have redeemed my heart.*

Then we invite Christ in. We ask Jesus to come into the emotion, the memory, this broken place within us. We give him permission; we give him access. We open the door to this particular place in our hearts. "If you hear me calling and open the door, I will come in"

(Rev. 3:20 NLT). Truth be told, there are probably many broken places within us. Stay with one at a time, the one connected with the event or the emotion or the habit you can't seem to escape. Ask Jesus to bring his light there. "For God, who said, 'Let light shine out of darkness,' made his light shine in our hearts" (2 Cor. 4:6). Ask him to make it clear to you. *What's going on here, Jesus? What is this all about? Shine your light in my heart.*

> *Jesus, I invite you into this broken place within me (this wound, this memory). I give you total access to my heart. Come, Lord, shine your light here. Reveal to me all that is going on here. What is this about, Jesus? Come and show me, meet me here, in this place.*

Sometimes he will take us back to a memory, a time and place where a shattering blow was given. Other times he will make us aware of a young place in our hearts. Just the other evening, Stasi and I were in the living room together, reading. She told me she had been sad for several days, but she wasn't sure why. There wasn't anything sad going on in her life—quite the contrary. It had been a good several weeks with many blessings. But as she prayed about it, tuned in to her heart, she became aware of a place in her heart that felt as if it was weeping. Anytime someone says, "I feel like there's this part of me . . . ," my radar lights up. We asked Jesus about it, and sure enough, there was a part of Stasi's heart, about seventeen years old, that was grieving. We asked Jesus to come in and lead us in prayer for this brokenness.

We ask Jesus what he is saying to this wounded part of us, listening, as Payne puts it, "for the healing word that God is always sending to the wounded." He will often bring words of love and kindness, or comfort, specifically to this place in our hearts: "You have the words of real life" (John 6:68 *The Message*). Sometimes he will ask a question: *Why are you frightened?* or *Will you let me heal you?* He is drawing this place in our hearts out from the shadows, out from hiding; he is bringing our brokenness into the place of assurance.

>*Jesus, come and lead me in healing this brokenness in my heart. Speak to me here, Lord. What are you saying to me? Give me ears to hear and eyes to see what you are revealing. Let no other voice speak but you, my Lord Jesus, and you alone.*

Now, I think it is safe to say that we all have mishandled these places in our hearts. We push them down, as I did. Or we turn to something or someone we hope will bring comfort, like food or sex. If we have done that, Jesus will often make that clear to us as we pray. As he does, we confess our sins, renounce them (often a great act of the will), and ask him to cleanse our hearts (1 John 1:9).

>*Jesus, forgive me for the ways I've mishandled my brokenness. You alone make me dwell in safety. Forgive me for all my self-protection and self-redemption, and for all my false comforters. (You'll want to renounce specific sins you are aware of here.) Cleanse my heart of every sin by your shed blood.*

Oftentimes these young and broken places have become sites of spiritual strongholds. (This will make a great deal more sense after you read the next chapter.) All of the streams flow together for our healing; we must use the stream of Warfare as well. Our sins give the Enemy a certain claim to our lives (Rom. 6:16). As we renounce any sin, we also renounce any claim we've given to Satan in our lives. This often comes in the form of "agreements"—Satan has suggested something to us, and we have said, "Yes." He might have said, *Don't ever trust anyone,* or *Your heart is bad—never show it to anyone,* or *You are dirty . . . lustful . . . addicted and never will get free.* Whatever we have agreed with, we renounce those agreements. We ask God to cleanse us by the blood of Christ; we command our Enemy to flee (James 4:7).

> *I now break every agreement I have made with Satan and his lies. (Get specific here. What have you believed, bought into?) I renounce any claim I have given to my Enemy, and in the name of Jesus I command him to flee.*

And then we ask Jesus to do for us the very thing he said he came to do: we ask him to heal this brokenness, to bind up our hearts. Sometimes he will ask us to take his hand in this shattered place, follow him into his heart and his presence within us. These places are often isolated from the life and the love of God in us; he draws them back into his presence and heals them through union with himself, *in* our hearts. Our part is to listen and follow where he is leading, and to welcome that part of our heart home. This is so important because many of us *sent* that part away. We welcome back the despised, forsaken part, just as Jesus embraces us.

> *Jesus, come now and do as you promised to do—heal my broken heart and set me free. (Listen here for what Jesus is saying.) Bring this place into your love and healing, bring this place home. I welcome your healing, and I welcome this part of my heart home. Come, bind me up and make me whole.*

CARRY ON THE JOURNEY

"Healing prayer," says Payne, "is not the 'instant fix,' nor the bypassing of slow and steady growth. It is that which clears the path and makes such progress possible." Brokenness keeps so many people from walking the path that God has for them. "Make straight paths for your feet, so that the limb which is lame may not be put out of joint, but rather be healed" (Heb. 12:13 NASB). As long as we have these unhealed places within us, these rifts in the soul, we will find it next to impossible to live in freedom and victory. No matter how much we demand of ourselves, applying discipline and doctrine, it will not work. It has not worked. Those places keep undermining us at crucial moments, cutting us off at the knees. And our Enemy knows them well and uses them against us with disabling effect. I'll say more about that in a moment. We desperately need the stream of Healing, so that we may go on to walk this journey with Christ.

> Then Gandalf said: "Let us not stay at the door, for the time is urgent. Let us enter! For it is only in the coming of Aragorn that any hope remains for the sick that lie in the House. Thus spake Ioreth, wise-woman of Gondor: *The hands of the king are the hands of a healer, and so shall the rightful king be known . . .*"
>
> Now Aragorn knelt by Faramir, and held a hand upon his brow. And those that watched felt that some great struggle was going on. For Aragorn's face grew grey with weariness; and ever and anon he called the name of Faramir, but each time more faintly to their hearing, as if Aragorn himself was removed from them, and walked afar in some dark vale, calling for one that was lost.
>
> And at last Bergil came running in, and he bore six leaves in a cloth. "It is kingsfoil, Sir," he said; "but not fresh, I fear. It must have been culled two weeks ago at the least. I hope it will serve, Sir?" Then looking at Faramir he burst into tears.
>
> But Aragorn smiled. "It will serve," he said. "The worst is now over. Stay and be comforted!" Then taking two leaves, he laid them on his hands and breathed on them, and then he crushed them, and straightaway a living freshness filled the room, as if the air itself awoke and tingled, sparkling with joy . . .
>
> Suddenly Faramir stirred, and he opened his eyes, and he looked on Aragorn who bent over him; and a light of knowledge and love was kindled in his eyes, and he spoke, softly. "My lord,

you called me. I come. What does the king command?" "Walk no more in the shadows, but awake!" said Aragorn . . . "I will, my lord," said Faramir. "For who would lie idle when the king has returned?" (J. R. R. Tolkien, *The Return of the King*)

CHAPTER NINE

Spiritual Warfare: Fighting for Your Heart

It is the image of God reflected in you that so enrages hell;
it is this at which the demons hurl their mightiest weapons.

—William Gurnall

Awake, awake, O Zion,
    clothe yourself with strength . . .
Shake off your dust;
    rise up, sit enthroned, O Jerusalem.
Free yourself from the chains on your neck,
    O captive Daughter of Zion.

—God (Isa. 52:1–2)

Wolfgang Amadeus Mozart was a glorious man. An image bearer. You remember from your youth the little song "Twinkle, Twinkle, Little Star"? Mozart wrote that melody when he was three. He composed his first symphony when he was twelve. And Mozart's music has *endured,* enchanting the world for centuries. He is probably played more often than any other classical composer. Yet this brilliant man died young—we don't really know how or why. Impoverished, alone, his body was dumped in a common grave. The movie *Amadeus* is Peter Shaffer's attempt to tell that tale.

It's a story of genius and jealousy, leading to murder. Shaffer creates a villain worthy of the devil himself in the character of the court composer Salieri. A musician of lesser note, Salieri is tormented by envy of Mozart's greatness. Like Joseph's brothers. He embodies what must have been Lucifer's jealousy of God's glory, which brought the angel to his ruin. There is a remarkable scene in the film that depicts the day Mozart's wife brings his music to Salieri, in hopes of getting her husband a job. She does not yet know that he is a wolf in sheep's clothing. Glancing through the pages of Mozart's portfolio, Salieri is captivated by the work of his rival's hand.

SALIERI: These . . . are *originals*?

FRAU MOZART: Yes, sir. He doesn't make copies.

[*As the astonished composer begins to read the sheets before him, he narrates the tale.*]

SALIERI: Astounding. It was actually . . . beyond belief. These were first, and *only* drafts of music. But they showed no correction of any kind. Not one. He had simply written down music already finished . . . in his *head!* Page after page of it, as if he were just taking dictation! And music . . . finished like no music is ever finished. Displace one note and there would be diminishment. Displace one phrase and the structure would fall. It was clear to me . . . that sound I had heard in the Archbishop's palace had been no accident. Here again was the very voice of God. I was staring through the cage of those meticulous ink strokes at an absolute beauty.

[*Salieri is enraptured, and the sheets fall to the floor from his limp hands.*]

FRAU MOZART: Is it not good?

SALIERI: [*Clearly wounded*] It is . . . miraculous.

FRAU MOZART: Yes . . . he's very proud of his work. So you will help us?

[*Sullen, determined, Salieri simply leaves the room in silence. The scene shifts to his private chambers. Salieri is taking down a crucifix from the wall and placing it in the fire.*]

SALIERI: From now on we are enemies, You and I. Because You choose for Your instrument a boastful, lustful, smutty, infantile boy . . . and give me only the ability to recognize the Incarnation. Because You are *unjust . . . unfair . . . unkind!* I will block You. I swear it. I will hinder and harm Your creature here on earth as far as I am able. [*Shaking his fist in the air*] I will ruin Your incarnation.

OUR SITUATION

This is the heart of our Enemy. He is determined to hinder and harm and ruin God's image bearers. To steal and kill and destroy. So, let me say this again: the story of your life is the story of the long and brutal assault on your heart by the one who knows what you could be and fears it. I hope you are beginning to see that more clearly now. Otherwise, much of the Bible will not make sense to you. Much of your *life* will not make sense to you.

> I will go before you
>> and will level the mountains;
> I will break down gates of bronze
>> and cut through bars of iron.
> I will give you the treasures of darkness,
>> riches stored in secret places,
> so that you may know that I am the LORD,
>> the God of Israel, who summons you by name. (Isa. 45:2–3)

Doesn't the language of the Bible sometimes sound . . . overblown? Really now—God is going to level mountains for us? We'd be happy if he just helped us get through the week. What's all that about breaking down gates of bronze and cutting through bars of iron? I mean, it sounds heroic, but, well, who's really in need of that? This isn't ancient Samaria. We'd settle for a parking place at the mall. Now, I like the part about treasures of darkness and riches stored in secret places—it reminds me of *Treasure Island* and Long John Silver and all that. What boy hasn't wanted to find buried treasure? And, in fact, those associations make the passage seem like fantasy as well—good poetry, meant to inspire. But not much more.

What if we looked at the passage through the eyes of the heart? That language makes perfect sense if we are living a reality on the mythic level of *Amadeus* or *The Lord of the Rings*. In those stories, gates must be broken down, riches are hidden in darkness, and precious friends must be set free. If we *are* in an epic battle, then the language of the Bible fits perfectly. Things are not what they seem. We are at war. That war is against your heart, your glory. Once more, look at Isaiah 61:1:

> He has sent me to bind up the brokenhearted,
> to proclaim freedom for the captives
> and release from darkness for the prisoners.

This is God's personal mission for his people; the offer is for us all. So, we must all be held prisoner to some form of darkness. We didn't know it—that's proof enough. In the darkness we can't see. And what is this hidden treasure? Our *hearts*—they are the treasures hidden by darkness. They are not darkness; they are *hidden* by darkness, pinned down, held away in secret places like a hostage held for ransom. Prisoners of war. That is a given. That is assumed. The question is not, *Are* we spiritually oppressed, but *Where* and *How?*

Think of it—why does every story have a villain?

Little Red Riding Hood is attacked by a wolf. Dorothy must face and bring down the Wicked Witch of the West. Qui-Gon Jinn and Obi-Wan Kenobi go hand to hand against Darth Maul. To release the captives of the Matrix, Neo battles the powerful "agents." Frodo is hunted by the Black Riders. (The Morgul blade that the Black Riders pierced Frodo with in the battle on Weathertop—it was aimed at his heart.) Beowulf kills the monster Grendel, and then he has to battle Grendel's mother. Saint George slays the dragon. The children who stumbled into Narnia are called upon by Aslan to battle the White Witch and her armies so that Narnia might be free.

Every story has a villain because *yours* does. You were born into a world at war. When Satan lost the battle against Michael and his angels, "he was hurled to the earth, and his angels with him" (Rev. 12:9). That means that right now, on this earth, there are hundreds of thousands, if not millions, of fallen angels, foul spirits, bent on our destruction. And what is Satan's mood? "He is filled with fury, because he knows that his time is short" (v. 12). So what does he spend every day and every night of his sleepless, untiring existence doing? "Then the dragon was enraged at the woman and went off to make war against . . . those who obey God's commandments and hold to the testimony of Jesus" (v. 17). He has you in his crosshairs, and he isn't smiling.

You have an Enemy. He is trying to steal your freedom, kill your heart, destroy your life. As Satan said through Salieri, "I will hinder and harm Your creature here on earth as far as I am able. I will ruin Your incarnation." Very, very few people live like that. The alarm goes off, and they hit the snooze button, catch a few extra winks, gulp down a cup of coffee on their way to work, wonder why there are so many hassles, grab some lunch, work some more, come home under a sort of cloud, look at the mail, have dinner, watch a little TV, feed the cat, and fall into bed—without once even wondering how the Enemy might be attacking them. All they know is, they sure aren't enjoying that abundant life Christ talked about.

To find the freedom and the life offered by Christ, we must live in all Four Streams. To be restored as a man or a woman fully alive, we must live in all Four Streams. This, the fourth, may be the most neglected of all. And frankly, it may be the most critical. To live in ignorance of spiritual warfare is the most naive and dangerous thing a person can do. It's like skipping through the worst part of town, late at night, waving your wallet above your head. It's like walking into an al-Qaida training camp, wearing an "I love the United States" T-shirt. It's like swimming with great white sharks, dressed as a wounded sea lion and smeared with blood. And let me tell you something: you don't escape spiritual warfare simply because you choose not to believe it exists or because you refuse to fight it.

The bottom line is, you are going to have to fight for your heart. Remember John 10:10—the thief is trying to steal the life God wants to give.

SUBTLE ATTACK—LOOKING FOR AGREEMENTS

The devil has more temptations than an actor has costumes for the stage. And one of his all-time favorite disguises is that of a lying spirit, to abuse your tender heart with the worst news he can deliver—that you do not really love Jesus Christ and that you are only pretending, you are only deceiving yourself. (William Gurnall)

Satan is called in Scripture the Father of Lies (John 8:44). His very first attack against the human race was to lie to Eve and Adam about God, and where life is to be found, and what the consequences of certain actions would and would not be. He is a master at this. He suggests to us—as he suggested to Adam and Eve—some sort of idea or inclination or impression, and what he is seeking is a sort of "agreement" on our part. He's hoping we'll buy into whatever he's saying, offering, insinuating. Our first parents bought into it, and look what disaster came of it. But that story is not over. The Evil One is still lying to us, seeking our agreement every single day.

Your heart is good. Your heart matters to God. These are the two hardest things to hang on to. I'm serious—try it. Try to hold this up for even a day. *My heart is good. My heart matters to God.* You will be amazed at how much accusation you live under. You have an argument with your daughter on the way to school; as you drive off, you have a nagging sense of, *Well, you really blew that one.* If your heart agrees—*Yeah, I really did*—without taking the issue to Jesus, then the Enemy will try to go for more. *You're always blowing it with her.* Another agreement is made. *It's true. I'm such a lousy parent.* Keep this up and your whole day is tanked in about five minutes. The Enemy will take any small victory he can get. It moves from *You did a bad thing* to *You are bad.* Or weak. Or ugly. Or prideful. You know how it goes. After a while it just becomes a cloud we live under, accept as normal.

My friend Aaron decided to get into shape. He went out and took a run. First, the Enemy tried discouragement to get him to quit. *Look how far you have to go. You can't do this—you'll die out there. Give it up.* Aaron thought, *Gee—it is a long way. I'm not sure I can do this.* But then he recognized what was going on and pressed into it. The attack became more personal, more vicious. He was running along, and he was hearing stuff like this: *You're just a fat pig. You always have been.* A gorgeous woman in fabulous shape approached from the other direction. *She'd never be attracted to a slob like you.* "By the time I got back to my car," he said, "it felt like I'd been assaulted. But this time, I knew what it was and I won. I made no agreements."

This sort of thing goes on all the time. But unlike Aaron, most of the time we don't recognize it as an attack. At first it tends to be vague—not voices in the head, not an obvious assault, but more of a "sense" we have, an impression, a feeling that comes over us. The power of *suggestion.* Now, if some demon were standing in front of us, telling us, "Here, drink this rat poison," we'd tell him where to go. But because we do not live as though we are at war, well, we just assume these impressions are our own, and we accept them, agree with them, live under them like slaves under a task master. Listen carefully: any movement toward freedom and life, any movement toward God or others, *will be opposed.* Marriage, friendship, beauty, rest—the thief wants it all. A. W. Tozer wrote:

> So, it becomes the devil's business to keep the Christian's spirit imprisoned. He knows that the believing and justified Christian has been raised up out of the grave of his sins and trespasses. From that point on, Satan works that much harder to keep us bound and gagged, actually imprisoned in our own grave clothes. He knows that if we continue in this kind of bondage . . . we are not much better off than when we were spiritually dead.

Sadly, many of these accusations will actually be spoken by Christians. Having dismissed a warfare worldview, they do not know who is stirring them to say certain things. The Enemy used David, who apparently wasn't watching for it, to do his evil: "Satan rose up against Israel and incited David to take a census of Israel" (1 Chron. 21:1). He tried to use Peter too. "From that time on Jesus began to explain to his disciples that he must go to Jerusalem and suffer many things . . . Peter took him aside and began to rebuke him. 'Never, Lord!' he said. 'This shall never happen to you!' Jesus turned and said to Peter, 'Get behind me, Satan!'" (Matt. 16:21–23). Heads up—these words will come from anywhere. Be careful what or who you are agreeing with.

The whole plan is based on agreements. When we make those agreements with the demonic forces suggesting things to us, we come under their influence. It becomes a kind of permission we give the Enemy, sort of like a contract. The bronze gates start clanging shut around us. I'm serious—maybe half the stuff people are trying to "work through" in counseling offices, or pray about in their quiet times, is simply agreements they've made with the Enemy. Some foul spirit whispers, *I'm such a stupid idiot,* and they agree with it; then they spend months and years trying to sort through feelings of insignificance. They'd end their agony if they'd treat it for the warfare it is, break the agreement they've made, send the Enemy packing.

If you are having trouble taking in all of this, let me ask you: Have you had this experience? Something bad happens, and you start telling yourself what a jerk you are. Do you really think the source of that is just you? Or God? Think about it this way: Who would take the most delight in it? Take it all real slow if you need to. Start by simply entertaining the notion that the source might be something besides your "low self-esteem."

I don't mean to suggest it's easy. This can get really nasty.

We've been looking for a house for four years. A long story, one we haven't time for here, but those have been four years of ups and downs and promises and hopes and finally, just this last Sunday afternoon, we found it. It was not only beautiful and private; it was perfect for holding the many fellowship events that are the center-piece of our community. A perfect fit for our family. The only prop-erty we'd seen that met our criteria and made our hearts beat faster, and it was vacant—we could move in immediately. After a long, hard journey, we found a place of rest, a respite from the battle. We wrote up what we thought would be a slam-dunk offer. As our agent drove to deliver our contract, he received a call that another offer came in before us by twenty minutes. Some agent in his office saw our offer and sneaked one in ahead of ours designed to beat us out.

It felt like a perfect setup. Our hearts were so hopeful, open, vul-nerable. I can equate it only to something like parents waiting for four years to adopt, and finally the opportunity opens for them. God says, *This is your turn. This is my gift to your hearts.* They are promised a baby, but on the day they are supposed to receive her, she's given to another couple. We really thought this house was a gift from God. Not getting it was a direct, intentional wound to our hearts. It wasn't just about a *house,* for heaven's sake. That sounds silly. It was about our relationship with God, our walk with him . . . and therefore, about all the other things in our lives that flow from that. The wound came in at the most intimate place of our lives—our walk with God.

And a whole lot of other crap rushed in as well. Just as sharks can smell blood in the water from miles away, the enemies of our souls smell woundedness, and they close in for the kill. Suddenly, betrayal felt true. *God has betrayed you.* Desolation felt true. *None of what you believe is true.* Apostasy, abandoning all faith felt true. *Why walk with God if you can't trust him?* We were reeling. Thoughts went through my heart about how to get out of this book contract because I can't write except out of my walk with God . . . and that had been pierced. Stasi was crying. Our middle son was crying. I felt like I'd been . . . hit by a truck.

If Jesus said the thief comes to steal and kill and destroy, well, then, why don't we think the thief ever *actually comes* to steal and kill and destroy? Good grief—the things people just roll over and accept as "God's will." The house was just the move to steal; the Enemy wanted to kill our hearts and destroy our faith and all that flows from it. I think that's nearly always true. The particular attack is not the issue; he'll steal anything to kill and destroy.

During an assault like that, you must remember: *make no agreements.* The Enemy will suggest all sorts of things. *You see— God doesn't care. You're not worth fighting for. Your heart doesn't matter. You can't trust him.* He is trying to kill your heart, destroy the glory of your life. It will feel hard—really hard, almost impossible—but whatever you do, make no agreements. You have to start there.

OPEN ASSAULT

Stephen came to us because he was at the end of his rope. I liked him right away. He was an honest, insightful man, earnestly seeking the life of God. At one time he had been an alive and passionate friend of Jesus. He wrote music, led worship in his church. He had a Bible study in his home. Many people received specific words of encouragement and guidance from God through Stephen. He shared his faith with anyone. He walked with God. But that was long ago. It had been years since he'd been able to write any music; worship was as dead as your great-great-grandmother. He could not pray, could not read the Bible, could not hear from God. This man had been taken out.

During the first few years of his ordeal, Stephen sought the streams he knew to seek. Asked his pastor for counseling. Tried his best to push through it with discipline and prayer. Went to conferences, tried to hear from God. Nothing. He thought maybe it was that whole "silence of God" thing, thought if he just waited it out, it would lift. It didn't. No, it sat there like a great weight upon his spirit, a stone someone had rolled over his heart. After five years he'd almost given up. Thank God, he turned to the stream of Warfare.

As Stephen told me his story, this is what emerged: in his younger years as a boy, he had taken some serious wounds of rejection, the first one coming at the age of three from his father. The result was a vow never to let anyone hurt him again. He did, however, keep his heart open to his mother, from whom he received mercy and kindness. They were friends. She was the only relational connection he had. Stephen came to Christ as a young man. Shortly after, his mother grew very ill. He prayed and prayed she would not die. You know what's coming. She did. Understandably, a sense of betrayal and abandonment rode in on the wings of that pain. But he hung in there with his faith.

He tried to reach out again and trust others, especially men. He knew he needed to have that place in his heart healed, and he bravely sought to enter into a few deep relationships with men he trusted and respected. There were three of them; two he considered mentors, one a close friend. Both mentors ended up having affairs, one of them with a woman in Stephen's home group. The wounds pierced deeply, and what do you suppose came with them? Yep: betrayal and abandonment. He sought direction from his pastor over one of the affairs; since the woman was in his fellowship, Stephen felt a burden to at least confront the two. His pastor wounded him again, suggesting that Stephen was prideful and arrogant, and was making up part of the story. More betrayal, more abandonment. The Enemy will arrange to have others do to you what he is doing to you.

If we could have seen what happened in the spiritual realm, I think we would have seen some foul spirit at work right from the beginning. Paul warns us in Ephesians: "Do not let the sun go down while you are still angry, and do not give the devil a foothold" (4:26–27). Paul is writing to Christians here, and he makes it clear that a believer can have a stronghold of Satan in his life. It's not just about anger; it can happen through all sorts of issues. The Devil will try to use your wounds and unresolved emotional issues to pin down your heart under a spiritual stronghold. The wounds we take are not accidental. It was no doubt at Satan's suggestion that Stephen made that first vow never to let anyone in. Clearly, he seized the opportunity of the death of Stephen's mom to bring in all those feelings and thoughts of betrayal and abandonment.

Now, it was Stephen who made the agreements with the Enemy. People make choices, and they are responsible before God for those choices. But through those agreements the Evil One secured a beachhead (a "foothold" in Paul's words), then waited for an opportunity to take even greater dominion. In Stephen's case, the unresolved hurt and betrayal were there, and the addition of the affairs was just what the Enemy needed; no doubt he had some hand in those as well. The bronze gates closed over Stephen's heart, now a treasure hidden in darkness.

THERE IS NO ESCAPING THIS WAR

Stephen's story is really quite common. Remember, when Jesus boiled his whole mission down to healing the brokenhearted and setting prisoners free from darkness, he was referring to *all* of us. Our modern, scientific, Enlightenment worldview has simply removed spiritual warfare as a practical category, and so it shouldn't surprise us that we can't see spiritual strongholds after we say they don't really exist. It took all Four Streams to set Stephen free, but the clincher was the stream of Warfare. I'll explain in the next chapter how we did it. Now, he is free, I'm grateful to say. His heart is back. A few months later he said to me, "If we hadn't used all Four Streams, I'd probably have lived the rest of my life in that prison."

And that's true, dear friends. He probably would have.

If you deny the battle raging against your heart, well, then, the thief just gets to steal and kill and destroy. Some friends of mine started a Christian school together a few years ago. It had been their shared dream for nearly all their adult lives. After years of praying and talking and dreaming, it finally happened. Then the assault came . . . but they would not see it as such. It was "hassles" and "misunderstanding" at first. As it grew worse, it became a rift between them. A mutual friend warned them of the warfare, urged them to fight it as such. "No," they insisted, "this is about *us*. We just don't see eye-to-eye." I'm sorry to say their school shut its doors a few months ago, and the two aren't speaking to each other. Because they refused to fight it for the warfare it was, they got taken out. I could tell you many, many stories like that.

There is no war is the subtle—but pervasive—lie sown by an enemy so familiar to us we don't even see him. For too long he has infiltrated the ranks of the church, and we haven't even recognized him.

THE RELIGIOUS SPIRIT

I was reading the prophet Jeremiah a few weeks ago when I ran across a passage that referred to God as "the Lord Almighty." To be honest, it didn't resonate. There's something too religious about the phrase; it sounds churchy, sanctimonious. The *Lawd Almiiiighty*. It sounds like something your grandmother would say when you came into her kitchen covered in mud. I found myself curious about what the *actual* phrase means in Hebrew. Might we have lost something in the translation? So I turned to the front of the version I was using for an explanation. Here is what the editors said:

> Because for most readers today the phrases "the Lord of hosts" and "God of hosts" have little meaning, this version renders them "the Lord Almighty" and "God Almighty." These renderings convey the sense of the Hebrew, namely, "he who is sovereign over all the 'hosts' (powers) in heaven and on earth, especially over the 'hosts' (armies) of Israel."

No, they don't. They don't even come close. The Hebrew means "the God of angel armies," "the God of the armies who fight for his people." *The God who is at war*. Does "Lord Almighty" convey "the God who is at war"? Not to me, it doesn't. Not to anyone I've asked. It sounds like "the God who is up there but still in charge." Powerful, in control. The God of angel armies sounds like the one who would roll up his sleeves, take up sword and shield to break down gates of bronze, and cut through bars of iron to rescue me. Compare "Joe is a good man who is in control" to "Joe is a Navy Seal." It changes the way you think about Joe and what he's up to. Why don't "most readers today" understand about the God of angel armies? Could it be because we have abandoned a warfare worldview? Who sold us that crock of sanctimonious puff-and-fluff?

For that matter, who has kept the new covenant so effectively under wraps that most Christians still believe their hearts are evil? It happened again just the other night—a leader in their church told friends of mine, in a very direct way, "The heart is desperately wicked." Dear God—they hold to that lie as a core doctrine of their *faith*. To say your heart is good still sounds like heresy. Whose PR campaign made that so effective?

Let me ask you another question: Who did Jesus tangle with more than any other group or type of person? Who started the rumors about him to try to discredit his ministry? Who kept trying to put him on the spot with their loaded questions? And when it became clear they could not shame or intimidate him back into place, where did the open opposition to Christ come from? Who paid Judas the thirty pieces of silver? Who got the crowd to yell for Barabbas when Pilate was ready to let Jesus go?

Religion and its defenders have always been the most insidious enemy of the true faith precisely because they are not glaring opponents; they are *impostors*. A raving pagan is easier to dismiss than an elder in your church. Before Jesus came along, the Pharisees ran the show. Everybody took what they said as gospel—even though it didn't sound like good news at all. But we wrestle not against flesh and blood. The Pharisees and their brethren down through the ages have merely acted—unknowingly, for the most part—as puppets, the mouthpiece of the Enemy.

Satan realized he couldn't stop the church. Oh, he tried. He arranged to have Jesus killed as a babe (Matt. 2:16). He tried to seduce him as a man. He tried to marginalize his message by having

the religious establishment discredit him. Finally, he had him crucified. It backfired. Badly. Then he tried to stop the young church
through intimidation and through death, having most of them
killed. It also backfired. So he turned to a backup plan. If you
can't beat 'em . . . join 'em. Infiltrate their ranks dressed as an
angel of light (Gal. 1:8). Then slowly bring a veil over all that is
good and beautiful and true. Take them captive through their
own religion.

Where are the Four Streams? The Religious Spirit has turned
discipleship into a soul-killing exercise of principles. Most folks
don't even know they can walk with God, hear his voice. The
Religious Spirit has stigmatized counseling as a profession for sick
patients, and so the wounds of our hearts never get healed. He's
taken healing away from us almost entirely so that we sit in pews as
broken people, feeling guilty because we can't live the life we're supposed to live. And he takes warfare and mocks it, stigmatizes it as
well so that most of the church knows almost nothing about how
to break strongholds, set captives free.

Finally, the Religious Spirit makes it next to impossible for a person to break free by spreading the lie that *there is no war*. Be honest.
How many Christians do you know who practice spiritual warfare
as a normal, necessary, daily part of the Christian life? Some of my
dearest friends pull back from this stream and sort of cast a concerned look over me when I suggest it's going on. Onward, Christian
soldiers, marching as to war? You've got to be kidding me. We gave
up the hymn not so much for reasons of musical fashion but
because we felt ridiculous singing it, as you do when asked to sing
"Happy Birthday" in a restaurant to a perfect stranger. We don't
sing it 'cause it ain't true. We have acquiesced. We have surrendered
without a fight.

We've exchanged that great hymn for a subtle but telling substitute, a song that is currently being taught to thousands of children

in Sunday school each week, which goes something like this (sung in a very happy, upbeat tune):

> I may never march in the infantry,
>   ride in the cavalry,
>   shoot the artillery,
> I may never fly over the enemy
>   but I'm in the Lord's army, yes, sir!

There is no battle and there is no war and there is no Enemy and your life is not at stake and you are not desperately needed this very hour, but you're in the Lord's army. Yes, sir. Doing *what?* may I ask.

The reason I bring this up is that if you want the real deal, if you want the life and freedom that Jesus offers, then you are going to have to break free of this religious fog in particular. "It is for freedom that Christ has set us free. Stand firm, then, and do not let yourselves be burdened again by a yoke of slavery" (Gal. 5:1). So here's a bottom-line test to expose the Religious Spirit: if it doesn't bring freedom and it doesn't bring life, it's not Christianity. If it doesn't restore the image of God and rejoice in the heart, it's not Christianity.

The ministry of Jesus is summarized by one of those who knew him best when Peter brings the gospel to the Gentiles: "God anointed Jesus of Nazareth with the Holy Spirit and power, and . . . he went around doing good and healing all who were under the power of the devil, because God was with him" (Acts 10:38). In 1 John 3:8 (NKJV), we read, "For this purpose the Son of God was manifested, that He might destroy the works of the devil." The stream of Spiritual Warfare was essential to Jesus' life and ministry. It follows that it must be essential to ours if we would be his followers.

CHAPTER TEN

SETTING HEARTS FREE: INTEGRATING THE FOUR STREAMS

Can plunder be taken from warriors,
    or captives rescued from the fierce?
But this is what the LORD says:
"Yes, captives will be taken from warriors,
    and plunder retrieved from the fierce;
I will contend with those who contend with you,
    and your children I will save.
I will make your oppressors eat their own flesh;
    they will be drunk on their own blood, as with wine.
Then all mankind will know
    that I, the LORD, am your Savior,
    your Redeemer, the Mighty One of Jacob.

—ISAIAH (49:24–26)

They were about twice our height, and armed to the teeth. Through the visors of their helmets their monstrous eyes shone with a horrible ferocity. I was in the middle position, and middle giant approached me. My eyes were busy with his armor, and I was not a moment in settling the mode of attack. I saw that his body-armor was somewhat clumsily made, and that the overlappings in the lower part had more play than necessary, and I hoped that, in a fortunate moment, some joint would open a little, in a visible and accessible part. I stood till he came near enough to aim a blow at me with the mace, which has been, in all ages, the favorite weapon of giants, when, of course, I leaped aside, and let the blow fall upon the spot where I had been standing. Full of fury, he made at me again; but I kept him busy, constantly eluding his blows, and hoping thus to fatigue him. He did not seem to fear any assault from me, and I attempted none as yet. At length, as if somewhat fatigued, he paused for a moment, and drew himself slightly up; I bounded forward, foot and hand, ran my rapier through to the armor of his back, let go the hilt, and passing under his right arm, turned as he fell, and flew at him with my saber. At one happy blow I divided the band of his helmet, which fell off, and allowed me, with a second cut across the eyes, to blind him. After which I clove his head.

I stood exhausted amidst the dead, after the first worthy deed of my life.

I searched the giants, and found the keys of their castle, to which I repaired . . . I released the prisoners, knights and ladies, all in a sad condition, from the cruelties of the giants. (George MacDonald, *Phantastes*)

FIERCE MASTERY

Let's come back for a moment to original glory, the glory of God given to us when we were created in his image. So much light could be shed on our lives if we would explore what we were *meant* to be before things started going wrong. What were we created to *do*? What was our original job description?

Then God said, "Let us make man in our image, in our likeness, and let them rule over the fish of the sea and the birds of the air, over the livestock, over all the earth, and over all the creatures that move along the ground." So God created man in his own image, in the image of God he created him; male and female he created them. God blessed them and said to them, "Be fruitful and increase in number; fill the earth and subdue it. Rule." (Gen. 1:26–28)

And let them *rule*. Like a foreman runs a ranch or like a skipper runs his ship. Better still, like a king rules a kingdom, God appoints us as the governors of his domain. We were created to be the kings and queens of the earth (small *k*, small *q*). Hebrew scholar Robert Alter has looked long and hard at this passage, mining it for its riches. He says the idea of *rule* means "a fierce exercise of mastery." It is active, engaged, passionate. It is *fierce*. I suppose such language doesn't really fit if we were created to spend our days singing in the choir ("I may never march in the infantry"). But it makes perfect sense if we were born into a world at war. God says, "It will not be easy going. This is no Sunday school hour. Rule fiercely in my name." We were meant to rule, as he—the God of angel armies—rules.

Now—what will be our role in the kingdom of God to come? What does he have in store for us in the future? Let's take the parable of the talents as one example. A landowner is going away for a while, and he appoints his servants to take care of the place while he's gone. Some do, and some don't. When he returns, he rewards those who ruled well in his absence by giving them even greater authority over his estate. He says, "Well done, good and faithful servant! You have been faithful with a few things; I will put you in charge of many things" (Matt. 25:21). Jesus teaches that in the coming kingdom, we will be promoted to positions of authority, and we will reign with him there. The ranch hand is promoted to foreman; the manager gets the vice president's office; the prince becomes king.

To drive the point home, Jesus follows this parable with another, a story about some sheep and goats. The sheep are the good guys in this tale, and their reward is really amazing. Jesus says, "Then the King will say to those on his right, 'Come, you who are blessed by my Father; take your inheritance, the kingdom prepared for you since the creation of the world'" (Matt. 25:34). He doesn't say, "Good job. Now, come and sing songs in heaven forever." He gives them an entire kingdom to rule over—a kingdom waiting for them since the beginning of time. That was the plan all along. That's why we read in Revelation 22:5, "And they [meaning the saints] will reign for ever and ever." We will rule, just as we were always meant to.

And in the meantime? What is God up to with us in the meantime? Training us to do what we're made to do: rule. In the gospel of Luke, chapter 10, there is a sort of test flight for this whole idea. Christ appoints seventy-two of his disciples—not the apostles, just regular folks like you and me—to go out and prepare the way for his ministry. (The story will make more sense if we remember that his ministry is healing the brokenhearted and setting the captives free.) Jesus sets the stage by saying, "I am sending you out like lambs among wolves" (10:3). In other words, this could get vicious. It's no rummage sale.

Now, when the seventy-two return, they are blown away by what happened: "The seventy-two returned with joy and said, 'Lord, even the demons submit to us in your name'" (10:17). Christ gives his followers his authority, and they go out to set captives free. Jesus listens carefully to the report, and then he says, "I saw Satan fall like lightning from heaven" (v. 18). In other words, "You see, you guys? It works! It *works*! Satan's days are numbered!" But the battle is not over; it's just beginning to heat up. Jesus then goes on to say, "I have given you authority to . . . overcome all the power of the enemy" (v. 19). There's more to be done. This was only a trial run. After his resurrection, Jesus sends us *all* out to do what he did: "As the Father has sent me, so I send you" (John 20:21 NRSV). And he gives us his authority to do it: "All authority in heaven and on earth has been given to me. Therefore go" (Matt. 28:18–19). Why else would he have given us his authority if we weren't supposed to *use* it?

The attitude of so many Christians today is anything *but* fierce. We're passive, acquiescent. We're acting as if the battle is over, as if the wolf and the lamb are now fast friends. Good grief—we're beating swords into plowshares as the armies of the Evil One descend upon us. We've bought the lie of the Religious Spirit, which says, "You don't need to fight the Enemy. Let Jesus do that." It's nonsense. It's unbiblical. It's like a private in Vietnam saying, "My commander will do all the fighting for me; I don't even need to fire my weapon." We are *commanded* to "resist the devil, and he will flee from you" (James 4:7). We are told, "Your enemy the devil prowls around like a roaring lion looking for someone to devour. Resist him" (1 Peter 5:8–9); "Fight the good fight" (1 Tim. 1:18); "Rescue those being led away to death" (Prov. 24:11).

Seriously, just this morning a man said to me, "We don't need to fight the Enemy. Jesus has won." *Yes,* Jesus has won the victory over Satan and his kingdom. *However,* the battle is not over. Look at 1 Corinthians 15:24–25: "Then the end will come, when he [Jesus] hands over the kingdom to God the Father after he has destroyed all dominion, authority and power. For he must reign until he has put all his enemies under his feet." *After* he has destroyed the rest of the Enemy's works. *Until* then, he must reign by bringing his enemies under his feet. Jesus is still at war, and he calls us to join him.

Leanne Payne recounts a story from the life of Catherine of Sienna that helped her see the battle for her heart and trained her to fight it. In the story, Catherine has gone up to a secret place to pray:

> As she began to pray, her ears were assaulted by blasphemous words, and she cried out to God, "Oh, look, Lord, I came up

here to give you my day. Now look what is happening." And the Lord said, "Does this please you, Catherine?" "Oh no, Lord," she said. And the Lord said, "It is because I indwell you that this displeases you so." These words brought instant understanding of my plight . . . I also knew that the problem was not a state or condition of my mind or my heart, but that it was harassment from without, from the accuser of my soul. I knew beyond all shadow of a doubt that "Greater is he who is in you, than he who is in the world." I then cried out to God, "Take it away, Lord. Send this filthy, horrible thing away." But the Lord said, "No, you do it." It was then that I learned spiritual authority. Centered in God and He in me, I took authority over the evil spirit when it manifested itself and commanded it to leave. After several months of this, a concentrated training in moving from the center where Christ dwells, I was utterly free of this harassment.

Notice, first, that the victory came when she realized that those awful thoughts were *not* from her; her heart is good. The assault came from *outside,* from the Enemy. That is the turning point, when we begin to operate as if the heart is good, and we are at war. Second, notice that Jesus told *her* to send it away. "You do it." *We* must exercise our authority in Christ. *We* are to resist. Finally, notice that it took several months of battle for a final victory. During that period of time, she was not blowing it, nor was God holding out on her. It was *training*. We are made to rule. We need to learn how. Spiritual warfare is a great deal of our training.

SETTING CAPTIVES FREE

Let me come back now to Stephen's story and use it to show how the Four Streams work together to set us free. You might recall that I asked Stephen to first tell me his story. We need to hear a person's story to get some understanding and context of what's going on in their heart and life. This is the stream of Counseling. I always listen carefully for the wounds, for how we mishandle them, and for where the Enemy has probably come in. Stephen's wounds had a clear theme to them (as do ours). In his case, it was betrayal and abandonment.

But there is another piece of evidence that we often overlook. As we began to help Stephen, there was a strong pull on me to drop him altogether, a vague but strong sense that felt like, *C'mon, John. This isn't worth it. You can't help him. Back off.* In other words, betray and abandon him. The Enemy will always try to get you to do to someone what he is doing to that person. I've seen this *so* many times. A woman came into my office and immediately I felt this pull toward lust and *Use her—she's available.* Her story centered around the wounds of sexual abuse. That's where the Enemy had a stronghold. A man came in with a deep wound of emasculation. *Despise him* was the pull, and it took a serious conscious effort not to do so. There is a gravitational field the Enemy creates around a person that pulls everyone in her life to do to her what he is doing to her. Heads up— it's not you, and being aware of it becomes a *very* helpful diagnostic.

We prayed and listened to God on behalf of Stephen—listening to God, walking with God throughout the entire process, as his disciples. Jesus confirmed that there were spirits of Betrayal and Abandonment pinning down his heart, along with a spirit of Desolation. (Anytime someone totally loses his sense of God, can't worship, can't pray, loses faith, Desolation is usually a part of things.)

Yes—spirits have personalities and specific functions. Michael (whose name means "who is like God?") is an archangel, the captain of the Lord's hosts, with special duties to protect God's people (Rev. 12:7; Dan. 10:13, 21). Gabriel's name means "strong man of God," and he is often given the role of messenger (Dan. 8:16; Luke 1:19, 26). Fallen angels have similar qualities, though twisted for evil. Jesus rebukes a "deaf and mute spirit" from a boy (Mark 9:25), and Legion from a tormented man (Mark 5:1–13). Paul casts out from a fortune-teller a spirit of divination (Acts 16:18).

Now I know—there is a great deal of debate today around the issue of a Christian's being "possessed" by a demon. I am not saying that Stephen was possessed. I am saying that there were spiritual enemies present in his life—set *against* him, trying to make an illegitimate claim over him. Paul teaches in Ephesians that unresolved emotional issues can create spiritual strongholds in our lives—"'In your anger do not sin: Do not let the sun go down while you are still angry, and do not give the devil a foothold" (4:26–27). The word means more than just "opportunity"; it conveys a place of influence, even strong influence. The New International Version and *The Message* translate it as "foothold"; the New Living Translation has it as "mighty foothold." Paul is not writing about non-Christians; he is clearly speaking to believers and he is making it clear that we can have demonic footholds in our lives.

That is why, before we could go after those enemies of Stephen's heart, he first had to confess his part in the mess. God honors our will (remember God's words to Catherine—"you do it"). Stephen had to renounce the vow he'd made as a young boy never to let anyone get close to him again. Childhood vows are very dangerous things; they act as major agreements with the Enemy, give him permission to enter some part of our lives. Stephen also had to confess the bitterness he held toward God for not saving his mother, and toward those two men who had betrayed him. (Bitterness is one example of "letting the sun go down" on an issue, and giving the devil a foothold). By bringing those sins under the blood of Christ, the Enemy lost his hold (Col. 2:13–15; Rev. 12:11).

Now, the apostle Peter teaches us, *we* are to resist the devil because he "prowls around like a roaring lion looking for someone to devour" (1 Peter 5:8). Not just tempt. *Devour.* That idea has a vicious connotation to it, as in "really harm." Maul. And Peter goes on to clarify that this "someone" includes Christians because he says we are to "resist him, standing firm in the faith, because you know that your brothers throughout the world are undergoing the same kind of sufferings" (v. 9). He is writing to Christians, and using other Christians as examples that we can and will be spiritually assaulted—sometimes in very vicious ways. We *must* resist.

It was time for us to get fierce. Time for the stream of Warfare. You'll notice that sometimes Jesus had to command foul spirits with a *stern* voice (Luke 4:35). In fact, when he first tried to deliver the man with Legion in him, the demon didn't leave—and *Christ* was doing the commanding! He had to get more information, in that case, the name and number of the demons present (Mark 5:1–13).

Now, I know—setting people free from demonic oppression might seem really weird to our modern, scientific world, but it has been a normal part of Christian ministry ever since Jesus modeled it for us. (Remember—things are not what they seem. We are at war.) The disciples made it an essential part of their ministry too. "Crowds gathered from the towns around Jerusalem, bringing their sick and those tormented by evil spirits, and all of them were healed" (Acts 5:16). The early church fathers saw it as an essential part of their ministry too. Listen to this prayer, one of many deliverance prayers penned by John Chrysostom, archbishop of Constantinople:

Satan, the Lord rebukes you by his frightful name! Shudder, tremble, be afraid, depart, be utterly destroyed, be banished! You who fell from heaven and together with you all evil spirits: every evil spirit of lust, the spirit of evil . . . an imaginative spirit, and encountering spirit . . . or one altering the mind of man. Depart swiftly from this creature of the Creator Christ our God! And be gone from this servant of God, from his mind, from his soul, from his heart, from his reins, from his senses, from all his members, that he might become whole and sound and free, knowing God.

Notice that St. John is rebuking foul spirits by name, on behalf of a believer ("this servant of God"). One at a time, we brought the authority of Jesus Christ, who is Lord, and the fullness of the Cross, Resurrection, and Ascension against all three foul spirits set against Stephen. We commanded them to release their claim on him, and to go to their judgment in the name of Jesus. After a fierce battle, they left. Stephen was free.

But that was not the end of the work for Stephen.

We then turned to the issue of his broken heart. We moved from the stream of Warfare to the stream of Healing, for to leave those places unhealed is only to invite the Enemy to return in another form, another day. We prayed with Stephen in the way I described at the end of Chapter 8, bringing the broken places into the healing presence of Jesus. It was dramatic, it was beautiful, and *it worked*. He is writing music again, hearing God's voice, and starting another fellowship group. He is free.

FIFTEEN MINUTES TO FREEDOM

With every morn my life afresh must break
The crust of self, gathered about me fresh;
That thy wind-spirit may rush in and shake
The darkness out of me, and rend the mesh
The spider-devils spin out of the flesh—
Eager to net the soul before it wake,
That it may slumberous lie, and listen to the snake.
(George MacDonald)

A few years ago, as Stasi and I really began to wake up and have our eyes opened to the spiritual battle raging against us and those we love, she said, "Quick little prayers just aren't going to do it any-more." I'm smiling and shaking my head as I recall this. How true it was; how true it has become. If we would do what Jesus did—heal all those who are under the power of the devil—and if we would find the life that he offers us, we have to fight for it. Fiercely. That is where we are now in this great Story.

All spiritual warfare follows the simple pattern given us in James 4:7: submit, and resist. We always start by submitting ourselves to Christ, and then resist whatever has come against us or against those we love. I've found that it is best to do this daily. There is a "dailyness" to our walk with Christ that follows these themes. So what I offer here is a walk through the prayer that Stasi and I, and our ministry team, pray every day. I'm going to unpack it for you as we go along, to help you understand why we pray this way. This is *not* a formula, but a model, an *example*. It might seem a bit more involved than the prayer most of us shoot up to God as we run out the door, but I promise you, this is fifteen minutes toward *freedom*! Quick little prayers aren't going to do it anymore.

First, we have to *choose* to abide in Christ. It's not something that happens automatically, and we can lose connection with our Head (Col. 2:19). Not a loss of salvation, but a loss of that intimate con-nection to the Vine through which we receive his life. Every morn-ing we bring our lives fully back to Christ and under his lordship. It's important that we consecrate our whole being to Christ—body (Rom. 12:1), soul (Luke 10:27), and spirit (1 Cor. 6:17).

My dear Lord Jesus, I come to you now to be restored in you—to renew my place in you, my allegiance to you, and to receive from you all the grace and mercy I so desperately need this day. I honor you as my sovereign Lord, and I surrender every aspect of my life totally and completely to you. I give you my body as a living sacrifice; I give you my heart, soul, mind, and strength; and I give you my spirit as well.

Okay. Having consecrated ourselves, we cleanse our lives with the blood of Christ—a very powerful weapon in this war. It washes us from our sins and the sins of others against us (1 John 1:9). It also disarms Satan (Rev. 12:11). Next, the whole spiritual realm works under authority, so as we take our place under the headship of Christ, we extend our authority and covering over those who are under us. You might remember that Jesus was astounded by the faith of the centurion: "I have not found anyone in Israel with such great faith" (Matt. 8:10). Do you know what it was that the commander understood? *Authority.*

I cover myself with your blood—my spirit, my soul, and my body. And I ask your Holy Spirit to restore my union with you, seal me in you, and guide me in this time of prayer. In all that I now pray, I include (my wife, and/or my children, by name). Acting as their head, I bring them under my authority and covering, and I come under your authority and covering. Holy Spirit, apply to them all that I now pray on their behalf.

The major ways we give claim to the Enemy in our lives are through sin and through making agreements with him. Most of our sins fall under the category of pride (independence from God, self-sufficiency) and idolatry (giving our devotion or our fear or any part of the heart to something other than God). In this part of the prayer we humble ourselves by declaring God's rightful place in our lives. And we ask him to search us so that we might confess any sin or agreement we've unknowingly made with our Enemy.

Dear God, holy and victorious Trinity, you alone are worthy of all my worship, my heart's devotion, all my praise and all my trust and all the glory of my life. I worship you, bow to you, and give myself over to you in my heart's search for life. You alone are Life, and you have become my life. I renounce all other gods, all idols, and I give

you the place in my heart and in my life that you truly deserve. I con-
fess here and now that it is all about you, God, and not about me.
You are the Hero of this story, and I belong to you. Forgive me, God,
for my every sin. Search me and know me and reveal to me any
aspect of my life that is not pleasing to you, expose any agreements I
have made, and grant me the grace of a deep and true repentance.

God is Trinity, and we must learn to relate to him as such. We begin with our Father, who has done so much for us in Jesus Christ. Part of the way the saints overcome the Evil One in Revelation 12:11 is by "the word of their testimony." It's so powerful to declare again what is true, what God is to us, and what he has done on our behalf. (There's so much Scripture in this prayer, I've added notes, which you'll find at the end of this chapter, so that it doesn't distract from the actual praying. But you'll find it worthwhile to go over the passages at some point.)

Heavenly Father, thank you for loving me and choosing me before
you made the world.[1] You are my true Father—my Creator, my
Redeemer, my Sustainer, and the true end of all things, including my
life. I love you; I trust you; I worship you. Thank you for proving
your love for me by sending your only Son, Jesus, to be my substitute
and representative.[2] I receive him and all his life and all his work,
which you ordained for me. Thank you for including me in Christ,[3]
for forgiving me my sins,[4] for granting me his righteousness,[5] for mak-
ing me complete in him.[6] Thank you for making me alive with
Christ,[7] raising me with him,[8] seating me with him at your right
hand,[9] granting me his authority,[10] and anointing me with your Holy
Spirit.[11] I receive it all with thanks and give it total claim to my life.

Now we turn to the Son and to his three great works on our behalf, starting with the Cross. There is so much more that the

Cross has accomplished than our forgiveness, but the constant barrage of the Enemy's lies wears us down over time, and we forget what is true. By entering into the work of Christ daily, we appropriate in a fresh way all he has already done for us. After all, Christ told us to take up our cross daily, for we must "put to death the misdeeds" of the flesh (Luke 9:23; Rom. 8:13).

> *Jesus, thank you for coming for me, for ransoming me with your own life.*[12] *I honor you as my Lord; I love you, worship you, trust you. I sincerely receive you as my redemption, and I receive all the work and triumph of your crucifixion, whereby I am cleansed from all my sin through your shed blood,*[13] *my old nature is removed,*[14] *my heart is circumcised unto God,*[15] *and every claim being made against me is disarmed.*[16] *I take my place in your cross and death, whereby I have died with you to sin and to my flesh,*[17] *to the world,*[18] *and to the Evil One.*[19] *I am crucified with Christ, and I have crucified my flesh with all its passions and desires.*[20] *I take up my cross and crucify my flesh with all its pride, unbelief, and idolatry. I put off the old man.*[21] *I now bring the cross of Christ between me and all people, all spirits, all things. Holy Spirit, apply to me (my wife and/or children) the fullness of the work of the crucifixion of Jesus Christ for me. I receive it with thanks and give it total claim to my life.*

Having put off the old man, we are told to put on the new (Eph. 4:24). The Resurrection astounded the first several centuries of the church; they saw it as central to living the Christian life. It's *life* that he promised, and it's *life* that we need. The Resurrection gives us that life. How awesome to begin to discover that through the power of the life of Christ in us, we *are* saved by his life (Rom. 5:10). We do, indeed, "reign in life" through him (Rom. 5:17).

Jesus, I also sincerely receive you as my new life, my holiness and sanctification, and I receive all the work and triumph of your resurrection, whereby I have been raised with you to a new life,[22] to walk in newness of life, dead to sin and alive to God.[23] I am crucified with Christ, and it is no longer I who live but Christ who lives in me.[24] I now take my place in your resurrection, whereby I have been made alive with you,[25] I reign in life through you.[26] I now put on the new man in all holiness and humility, in all righteousness and purity and truth. Christ is now my life,[27] the one who strengthens me.[28] Holy Spirit, apply to me (my wife and/or my children) the fullness of the resurrection of Jesus Christ for me. I receive it with thanks and give it total claim to my life.

Finally, we turn to the ascension of Christ, whereby he was given all authority in heaven and earth. By the grace of God, we share that authority with Jesus. It was Adam who gave it away, and it was Christ who won it back. Satan and his emissaries bank an awful lot of their work on the fact that Christians don't know the power and authority we now have in Christ. When we begin to exercise that fierce mastery, everything begins to change.

Jesus, I also sincerely receive you as my authority and rule, my everlasting victory over Satan and his kingdom, and I receive all the work and triumph of your ascension, whereby Satan has been judged and cast down,[29] his rulers and authorities disarmed,[30] all authority in heaven and on earth given to you, Jesus,[31] and I have been given fullness in you, the Head over all.[32] I take my place in your ascension, whereby I have been raised with you to the right hand of the Father and established with you in all authority.[33] I bring your authority and your kingdom rule over my life, my family, my household, and my domain.

And now I bring the fullness of your work—your cross, resurrection, and ascension—against Satan, against his kingdom, and against all his emissaries and all their work warring against me and my domain. Greater is he who is in me than he who is in the world.[34] *Christ has given me authority to overcome all the power of the Evil One, and I claim that authority now over and against every enemy, and I banish them in the name of Jesus Christ.*[35] *Holy Spirit, apply to me (my wife and my children) the fullness of the work of the ascension of Jesus Christ for me. I receive it with thanks and give it total claim to my life.*

Now we turn to the third member of the Trinity, the Holy Spirit. For as the Bible says, "Now the Lord is the Spirit, and where the Spirit of the Lord is, there is freedom" (2 Cor. 3:17). We want all of the freedom that the Spirit of God gives to us, and we want all of his work in our lives. So we honor him as Lord, and choose to walk in step with him at all times. You don't have to be Pentecostal to appreciate all that the Holy Spirit was meant to be toward us. Personally, I don't consider myself a charismatic, but I do need and want all that the Spirit of God offers me. After all, Christ sent him to us . . . at pentecost (Acts 2).

Holy Spirit, I sincerely receive you as my Counselor, my Comforter, my Strength, and my Guide.[36] *Thank you for sealing me in Christ.*[37] *I honor you as my Lord, and I ask you to lead me into all truth, to anoint me for all of my life and walk and calling, and to lead me deeper into Jesus today.*[38] *I fully open my life to you in every dimension and aspect—my body, my soul, and my spirit— choosing to be filled with you, to walk in step with you in all things.*[39] *Apply to me, blessed Holy Spirit, all of the work and all of the gifts in pentecost.*[40] *Fill me afresh, blessed Holy Spirit. I receive you with thanks and give you total claim to my life (and my wife and/or children).*

Having given the triune God his rightful place in our lives, and having received all that God has done for us, we turn now to some final preparations for the day:

Heavenly Father, thank you for granting to me every spiritual blessing in the heavenlies in Christ Jesus.[41]

I receive those blessings into my life today, and I ask the Holy Spirit to bring all those blessings into my life this day. Thank you for the blood of Jesus. Wash me once more with his blood from every sin and stain and evil device. I put on your armor—the belt of truth, the breastplate of righteousness, the shoes of the readiness of the gospel of peace, the helmet of salvation. I take up the shield of faith and the sword of the Spirit, the Word of God, and I wield these weapons against the Evil One in the power of God. I choose to pray at all times in the Spirit, to be strong in you, Lord, and in your might.[42]

Father, thank you for your angels. I summon them in the authority of Jesus Christ and release them to war for me and my household.[43] *May they guard me at all times this day. Thank you for those who pray for me; I confess I need their prayers, and I ask you to send forth your Spirit and rouse them, unite them, raising up the full canopy of prayer and intercession for me.*[44] *I call forth the kingdom of the Lord Jesus Christ this day throughout my home, my family, my life, and my domain. I pray all of this in the name of Jesus Christ, with all glory and honor and thanks to him.*

We've been praying along these lines for several years now. Every time we do it's like a fog lifting—the clouds break, and suddenly, faith is obvious, God is near, we see again, and we can breathe. Give it a week or two—you'll see. (For your convenience, the prayer has been duplicated at the back of this book, intact and without footnotes.) Walking in the stream of Warfare will draw you close to Christ, for there is no other safe place to abide. It will make you holy because you'll find that the Enemy will try to seize any open door—sort of like a presidential campaign. They look for "dirt" on you, go through old files. As the attack comes, it causes you to sanctify yourself even more deeply, close those doors, break those agreements. And it will deepen your appreciation for the work of Christ on your behalf. He has not left you on your own; he *did* come through. Mightily.

In the second film of *The Lord of the Rings* trilogy—*The Two Towers*—there is a king who is reluctant to go to war. Theoden, lord of the horse warriors of Rohan, is fearful and timid. An army is marching through his lands, an army bred for a single purpose: to destroy the world of men. Villages fall; women and children are slain. Still Theoden balks: "I will not risk open war." "Open war is upon you," says Aragorn, "whether you would risk it or not." As I watched this scene I could not help thinking of the church. It made me so sad. I love the Bride of Christ. I hate to see her captive in any way. *The primary reason* most people do not know the freedom and life Christ promised is that they won't fight for it, or they have been told not to fight for it. Friends, we are now in the midst of an epic battle, a brutal and vicious war against an Enemy who knows his time is short. Open war is upon you, whether you would risk it or not.

Notes

1. Ephesians 1:4.
2. Romans 5:8.
3. 1 Corinthians 1:30.
4. Colossians 2:13.
5. 2 Corinthians 5:21.
6. Colossians 2:10.
7. Colossians 2:13.
8. Colossians 3:1.
9. Ephesians 2:6.
10. Luke 10:19; Ephesians 2:6.

11. Ephesians 1:13.

12. Matthew 20:28.

13. 1 John 1:9.

14. Colossians 2:11.

15. Romans 2:29.

16. Colossians 2:15.

17. Romans 6:11.

18. Galatians 6:14.

19. Colossians 1:13.

20. Galatians 2:20.

21. Ephesians 4:22.

22. Romans 6:4.

23. Romans 6:11.

24. Galatians 2:20.

25. Ephesians 2:5.

26. Romans 5:17.

27. Colossians 3:4.

28. Philippians 4:13.

29. John 12:31.

30. Colossians 2:15.

31. Matthew 28:18.

32. Colossians 2:10.

33. Ephesians 2:6.

34. 1 John 4:4.

35. Luke 10:19.

36. John 14:16; Acts 9:31.

37. Ephesians 1:13.

38. John 15:26; 16:13.

39. Galatians 5:25.

40. Ephesians 4:8.

41. Ephesians 1:3.

42. Ephesians 6:10–18.

43. Hebrews 1:14.

44. 2 Corinthians 1:8–11.

PART FOUR

THE WAY OF THE HEART

Rise, heart
Thy Lord is risen.
—GEORGE HERBERT

If all of this is true (and it is true), there are some deep and urgent implications. Many of those have probably begun to occur to you already. But there are two I must unveil.

You might remember that the first Christians were called "followers of the Way" (Acts 9:2; 18:25–26). They had found the Way of Life and had given themselves over to it. They lived together, ate together, fought together, celebrated together. They were intimate allies; it was a fellowship of the heart. How wonderful it would be if we could find the same. How dangerous it will be if we do not.

Finally, let me ask you a question: How would you live differently if you believed your heart was the treasure of the kingdom? Because we are at war, the business of guarding the heart is a most serious business indeed. It is precisely because we do not know what the next turn of the page will bring that we nourish our hearts *now*, knowing at least this much: we will need our whole hearts for whatever is coming next. Above all else, you must care for your heart. For without your heart . . . well, have a look around.

CHAPTER ELEVEN

FELLOWSHIPS OF THE HEART

All the believers were one in heart.

—LUKE THE PHYSICIAN (ACTS 4:32)

Elrond summoned the hobbits to him. He looked gravely at Frodo. "The time has come," he said.

"The Company of the Ring shall be Nine; and the Nine Walkers shall be set against the Nine Riders that are evil. With you and your faithful servant, Gandalf will go; for this shall be his great task, and maybe the end of his labors. For the rest, they shall represent the other Free Peoples of the World: Elves, Dwarves, and Men. Legolas shall be for the Elves; and Gimli son of Glóin for the Dwarves. They are willing to go at least to the passes of the Mountains, and maybe beyond. For men you shall have Aragorn son of Arathorn, for the Ring of Isildur concerns him closely."

"Strider!" cried Frodo. "Yes," he said with a smile. "I ask leave once again to be your companion, Frodo." "I would have begged you to come," said Frodo, "only I thought you were going to Minis Tirith with Boromir." "I am," said Aragorn. "And the Sword-that-was-Broken shall be re-forged ere I set out to war. But your road and our road lie together for many hundreds of miles. Therefore Boromir will also be in the Company. He is a valiant man."

"There remain two more to be found," said Elrond. "These I will consider. Of my household I may find some that it seems good for me to send." "But that will leave no place for us!" cried Pippin in dismay. "We don't want to be left behind. We want to go with Frodo." "That is because you do not understand and cannot imagine what lies ahead," said Elrond. "Neither does Frodo," said Gandalf, unexpectedly supporting Pippin. "Nor do any of us see clearly. It is true that if these hobbits understood the danger, they would not dare to go. But they would still wish to go, or wish they had dared, and be shamed and unhappy. I think, Elrond, that in this matter it would be well to trust rather to their friendship than to great wisdom."

"Let it be so, then. You shall go," said Elrond, and he sighed. "Now the tale of Nine is filled. In seven days the Company must depart." (J. R. R. Tolkien, *The Fellowship of the Ring*)

WE HAPPY FEW

Once more, lend a mythic eye to your situation. Let your heart ponder this:

You awake to find yourself in the midst of a great and terrible war. It is, in fact, our most desperate hour. Your King and dearest Friend calls you forth. Awake, come fully alive, your good heart set free and blazing for him and for those yet to be rescued. You have a glory that is needed. You are given a quest, a mission that will take you deep into the heart of the kingdom of darkness, to break down gates of bronze and cut through bars of iron so that your people might be set free from their bleak prisons. He asks that you heal them. Of course, you will face many dangers; you will be hunted.

Would you try to do this *alone*?

Something stronger than fate *has* chosen you. Evil *will* hunt you. And so a fellowship *must* protect you. Honestly, though he is a very brave and true hobbit, Frodo hasn't a chance without Sam, Merry, Pippin, Gandalf, Aragorn, Legolas, and Gimli. He has no real idea what dangers and trials lie ahead. The dark mines of Moria; the Balrog that awaits him there; the evil orcs called the Urak-hai that will hunt him; the wastes of the Emyn Muil. He will need his friends. And you will need yours. You must cling to those you have; you must search wide and far for those you do not yet have. *You must not go alone.* From the beginning, right there in Eden, the Enemy's strategy has relied upon a simple aim: divide and conquer. Get them isolated, and take them out.

When Neo is set free from the Matrix, he joins the crew of the *Nebuchadnezzar*—the little hovercraft that is the headquarters and ship of the small fellowship called to set the captives free. There are nine of them in all, each a character in his own way, but nonetheless a company of the heart, a "band of brothers," a family bound together in a single fate. Together, they train for battle. Together, they plan their path. When they go back into the Matrix to set others free, each one has a role, a gifting, a glory. They function as a team. And they watch each other's back. Neo is fast, really fast, but he still would have been taken out if it hadn't been for Trinity. Morpheus is more gifted than them all, but it took the others to rescue him.

You see this sort of thing at the center of every great story. Dorothy takes her journey with the Scarecrow, the Tin Woodman, the Lion, and of course, Toto. Prince Caspian is joined by the last few faithful Narnians, and together they overthrow the wicked king Miraz. Though in the eyes of the world they are only gladiator-slaves, walking dead men, Maximus rallies his little band and triumphs over the greatest empire on earth. When Captain John Miller is sent deep behind enemy lines to save Private Ryan, he goes in with a squad of eight rangers. And, of course, Jesus had the Twelve. This is written so deeply on our hearts: *You must not go alone.* The Scriptures are full of such warnings, but until we see our desperate situation, we hear it as an optional religious assembly for an hour on Sunday mornings.

Think again of Frodo or Neo or Caspian or Jesus. Imagine you are surrounded by a small company of friends who know you well (characters, to be sure, but they love you, and you have come to love them). They understand that we all are at war, know that the purposes of God are to bring a man or a woman fully alive, and are living by sheer necessity and joy in the Four Streams. They fight for you, and you for them. Imagine you *could* have a little fellowship of the heart. Would you want it if it were available?

This Is Available

Leigh was born to dance.

But the story of her life is the story of that glory assaulted, stolen, and given up for lost. (This is *always* the story.) She was actually the first woman ever to win a scholarship to her university for dance. That might tell you how gifted she is. But talent alone is never enough to overcome wounds, and brokenness, and whatever hell has thrown at you from your childhood. Shame and Judgment hunted Leigh from her youth; they seemed larger than her heart to dance. She dropped out of school, married, had children, went on with her life. Still, the longing would not go away. When no one else was

around, Leigh would dance alone in her house, like a writer compos-
ing poetry from prison, or like a dolphin swimming round and round
its tank in captivity. From behind those infamous gates and bars,
Leigh's heart cried out to be free to do what she was meant to do.

Thirty years of seclusion went by. Thirty. Then Leigh took a risk.
She joined the dance ministry of her church. And she shone. Even
though she's old enough by now to be the mother of the other
dancers, Leigh stood out. She shone so much, in fact, that others
were threatened by her glory. You can hear it coming. Remember
Joseph's brothers? Cinderella's stepsisters? Satan seized the opportunity—accused Leigh of "pride" in the hearts of some of the members of the team, who turned on Leigh and shamed her openly.
(The attack always comes to "your heart is bad.") Not wanting to
be a source of strife, Leigh withdrew.

It became more and more obvious to us that Leigh would never
step into her glory unless someone fought for her. Fiercely. Over
the years her husband, Gary, fought valiantly for her, but more was
needed. Jesus reassures us: "I tell you the truth, whatever you bind
on earth will be bound in heaven . . . if two of you on earth agree"
(Matt. 18:18–19). Off and on, over the course of maybe a year, we
battled spiritual warfare for Leigh. One Saturday morning three of
us men spent more than three hours coming against her tormen-
tors, who were strong. Shame was there. So was Judgment. On
another night Stasi had a vision of a huge serpent binding Leigh's
feet. Aaron sent it to hell. Can captives be rescued from "the fierce"
(Isa. 49:24)? You betcha.

Leigh persevered. During our evenings together, there arose opportunities for prayer for the healing of childhood memories, too, and
the mending of her broken heart. This all took place in the normal
life of our community. At another point the women gathered to
celebrate Leigh's birthday. Their gift: dance shoes (something she
could never bring herself to spend money on). Their words of love

and encouragement might have been the greater gift, though. "You can do this, Leigh. We are for you." Those words meant something because they *knew* her. Words of life. Then, from within the fellowship, an opportunity came up for Leigh to dance—solo—before two thousand people. Understandably . . . she hesitated. Should she take the risk again? Was it a setup for disaster?

Leigh asked us to pray and listen to God on her behalf. *Is this the one, Lord?* It's so hard to hear from God when your own story is tangled up in it, and the Enemy has long assaulted the very thing you are wondering about. *Yes, it is time.* As Leigh practiced for the Big Day, she continued to be assaulted. She lost the rehearsal room. Her choreographer bailed. She pulled a hamstring. One physical injury after another. The Enemy laughed and mocked and threw the book at her. But her fellowship would not let her go. We slew the orcs; we found the trail; we stuck together.

After all those years, Leigh finally danced.

And she was glorious. I mean, it was *powerful.* Her performance launched other opportunities to dance. And *it would not have happened* without her friends.

I could fill a book with stories like that one, involving each member of our fellowship and the way we live in the Four Streams on behalf of one another. It's really quite normal, as ordinary as sending out for Chinese food or chatting on the phone.

It Must Be Small

When he left Rivendell, Frodo didn't head out with a thousand Elves. He had eight companions. Jesus didn't march around backed by hundreds of followers, either. He had twelve men—knuckleheads, every last one of them, but they were a band of brothers. This is the way of the kingdom of God. Though we are part of a great company, we are meant to live in little platoons. The little companies we form must be small enough for each of the members to know one another as friends and allies. Is it possible for five thousand people who gather for an hour on a Sunday morning to really and truly *know* each other? Okay, how about five hundred? One hundred and eighty? It can't be done. They can't possibly be intimate allies. It can be inspiring and encouraging to celebrate with a big ol' crowd of people, but who will fight for your heart?

Who will fight for your heart?

How can we offer the stream of Counseling to one another unless we actually *know* one another, know one another's stories? Counseling became a hired relationship between two people primarily because we couldn't find it anywhere else; we haven't formed the sort of small fellowships that would allow the stream to flow quite naturally. Is it possible to offer rich and penetrating words to someone you barely know, in the lobby of your church, as you dash to pick up the kids? And what about warfare? Would you feel comfortable turning to the person in the pew next to you and, as you pass the offering plate, asking him to bind a demon that is sitting on your head?

Where will you find the Four Streams?

The Four Streams are something we learn, and grow into, and offer one another, within a small fellowship. We hear each other's stories. We discover each other's glories. We learn to walk with God together. We pray for each other's healing. We cover each other's back. This small core fellowship is the essential ingredient for the Christian life. Jesus modeled it for us *for a reason*. Sure, he spoke to the masses. But he *lived* in a little platoon, a small fellowship of friends and allies. His followers took his example and lived this way too: "They broke bread in their homes and ate together with glad and sincere hearts" (Acts 2:46); "Aquila and Priscilla greet you warmly in the Lord, and so does the church that meets at their house" (1 Cor. 16:19); "Give my greetings to the brothers at Laodicea, and to Nympha and the church in her house" (Col. 4:15).

Church is not a building. Church is not an event that takes place on Sundays. I know, it's how we've come to think of it. "I go to First Baptist." "We are members of St. Luke's." "Is it time to go to church?" Much to our surprise, that is *not* how the Bible uses the term. Not at all. Certainly, the body of Christ is a vast throng, millions of people around the globe. But when Scripture talks about church, it means *community*. The little fellowships of the heart that are outposts of the kingdom. A shared life. They worship together, eat together, pray for one another, go on quests together. They hang out together, in each other's homes. When Peter was sprung from prison, "he went to the house of Mary the mother of John" where the church had gathered to pray for his release (Acts 12:12).

Anytime an army goes to war or an expedition takes to the field, it breaks down into little platoons and squads. And *every* chronicle of war or quest will tell you that the men and women who fought so bravely fought *for each other*. That's where the acts of heroism and sacrifice take place because that's where the devotion is. You simply cannot be devoted to a mass of people; devotion takes place in small units, just as in a family.

> We have stopped short of being an organization; we are an organism instead, a living and spontaneous association of individuals who know one another intimately, care for each other deeply, and feel a kind of respect for one another that makes rules and bylaws unnecessary. A group is the right size, I would guess, when each member can pray for every other member, individually and by name.

The preceding is the wisdom of Brother Andrew, who smuggled Bibles into Communist countries for decades. It's the model, frankly, of the church in nearly every country but the U.S. Now, I'm not suggesting you not do whatever it is you do on Sunday mornings. I'm simply helping you accept reality—whatever else you do, you *must* have a small fellowship to walk with you and fight with you and bandage your wounds. Remember, the path is narrow, and *few* find it. *Few* means "small in number," as opposed to, say, massive. This is essential. This is what the Scriptures urge us to do. First. Foremost. Not as an addition to Sunday. *Before* anything else.

IT MUST BE INTIMATE

Of course, small groups have become a part of the programming that most churches offer their people. For the most part, they are short-lived. There are two reasons. First, you can't just throw a random group of people together for a twelve-week study of some kind and expect them to become intimate allies. The sort of devotion we want and need takes place within a shared life. Over the years our fellowship has gone camping together. We play together; help one another move; paint a room; find work. We throw great parties. We fight for each other, live in the Four Streams. This is how it was meant to be.

I love this description of the early church: "All the believers were one in heart" (Acts 4:32). A camaraderie was being expressed there, a bond, an esprit de corps. It means they all loved the same thing, they all wanted the same thing, and they were bonded together to find it, come hell or high water. And hell or high water *will* come, friends, and this will be the test of whether or not your band will make it: if you are one in heart. Judas betrayed the brothers because his heart was never really with them, just as Cipher betrays the company on the *Nebuchadnezzar* and as Boromir betrays the fellowship of the Ring. My goodness—churches split over the size of the parking lot or what instruments to use during worship. Most churches are *not* "one in heart."

Second, most small groups are anything but redemptive powerhouses because, while the wineskin might be the right size, they don't have the right wine. You can do some study till you're blue in the face, and it won't heal the brokenhearted or set the captives free. We come; we learn; we leave. It is not enough. Those hearts remain buried, broken, untouched, *unknown*. It is the Way of the Heart and the Four Streams that turns a small fellowship into a redemptive community. It is knowing that you are at war, that God has chosen you and evil is hunting you, and so a fellowship like Frodo's must protect you. How many small groups have you been a part of where what we did for Leigh is what happens all the time?

On a Tuesday evening last January, those of us in our fellowship were sitting around talking about our need to see the rest of the picture, how we cannot make good decisions or even know what's really going on without eyes to *see*. That led into a conversation about the power of myth to open the eyes of our hearts. I suggested we do this: "Write down on a piece of paper five words or phrases that capture your life right now. What does it feel like? Don't edit. Don't make it sound better than it is. How are you doing?" It began an incredibly eye-opening journey.

Once we had our words or phrases (many of us couldn't keep it to five), I then asked, "What stories or scenes or characters help you *interpret* those words, help you see what's going on, give a context to your words for your life right now?" You see, no experience or feeling provides its own interpretation. You feel besieged on all sides. Are you Elijah on Mount Carmel, on the brink of great victory? Or are you Paul in Thessalonica, and you'd better get out of town, *fast*? We have to find something that gives our experiences meaning and context. And that's when the really good stuff took place. First, we shared our words and the stories that we felt interpreted them for us. Then, the fellowship offered to each other the characters and scenes that *we* saw for each other.

Misty had moved to our community a year earlier and had gone through a pretty tough time. New apartment, new job, all that.

Would she fit in? Does she really have anything to offer? Her words were: "Newness, uncharted territory, yellow brick road, fighting, a page turned, warfare." She thought that, maybe, there *might* be some truth for her in Dorothy from *The Wizard of Oz,* at least early in the story: "She sees things in others and calls them forth, but she's desperate to come home." The other story Misty chose felt more true; she really felt like the young woman in *Ever After* who "poses as royalty to save a servant friend, but she is exposed as less than royalty." As we listened first to her words and then to her interpretation, we all quietly jotted down our own stories for her.

When it was our chance to offer comments, five different people said, "Arwen," from *The Lord of the Rings.* It fit perfectly. She is beautiful (what woman doesn't long to hear this?), she is a warrior, and she is regal. And that is so true of Misty—all of it. Three folks also chose Dorothy from *Oz;* not because she's lost, but because she is right where she needs to be, and especially because she has a heart of gold. (By this point Misty is in tears. Did I mention she moved here from *Kansas?*) Then a real home run came—at least two of us offered Joan of Arc. I was one of them, and I had no idea where it came from. Misty was speechless. "I'm reading a book on her life right now. She's who I so *want* to be." God was speaking. What made it so powerful was that we saw her, she knew she was exposed to us, and what we saw was her glory. She felt called into something Great and Weighty, with beauty and courage to match.

"Longing, fear, lonely, waiting, thwarted." Those were Aaron's words. He chose Boromir from *The Fellowship of the Ring* "because he's the one that gets taken out, he's unstable, a mess." Aaron has fought a long, hard battle against a lot of oppression—some pretty fierce stuff. And his deep brokenness has often made him feel like he's just a mess. It's not true—but you know how when you're in need, it feels so shameful, like you're always in need. There was a moment of silence. Then every last one of us said, almost in the same breath, "Strider—Aragorn." Early in the story, isn't he also longing, lonely, waiting, thwarted? Aaron was speechless. "You're a good man, Aaron. You've walked a lonely trail, fought many hard battles. But your heart is good. You *are* Strider." Very, very quietly, like the dawn, he said, "That's who I want to be."

Stasi's words for her life were "persevering, hidden, misunderstood, weary, mundane tasks." She chose Lucy from *The Lion, the Witch and the Wardrobe* "because she wants to be faithful and true." (You'll recall that Lucy was also rather plain and not too pretty.) She also wrote down Lucilla, the empress in *Gladiator,* "because I long to be a beautiful, courageous empress." Notice that nearly always *our* interpretation of our days will reveal what we long to be but fear we really are not. Then it was our turn. Someone offered Cinderella, and *everyone* said, "Oh, my gosh. Yes!" She, too, was persevering, hidden, misunderstood, given mundane tasks. But she was also beautiful and didn't know it. We know Stasi's story; her glory *has* been assaulted. Remember how the wicked stepsisters tore the gown off Cinderella, so she couldn't go to the ball? I reminded Stasi of the time her sisters actually did that very thing to her. She burst into tears. "I forgot all about that . . . Oh, my." The truth was reaching her heart.

It was an incredible evening. All of us had chosen words that were hard (life is *hard*), and all our interpretations of our own lives were off. Each of us was in the process of making subtle agreements with the Enemy, and we weren't even aware of it. It was only through the eyes of our friends that we recovered our hearts, our true place, reality. But the real power of living in community is, we remembered those stories for months, and we used them for each other at crucial moments in the battle ahead. Jenny later said, "What makes this community so powerful is that you remember my story for me. I don't have to carry the burden of remembering alone." I tell you about that night because that's the kind of intimacy you need. It wouldn't have been possible to offer that to one another in a larger gathering. We need *intimate* allies.

It Will Be Messy

The family is . . . like a little kingdom, and, like most other little kingdoms, is generally in a state of something resembling anarchy.

G. K. Chesterton could have been talking about a little fellowship (our *true* family, because it is the family of God). It is a royal mess. I will not whitewash this. It is *disruptive*. Going to church with hundreds of other people to sit and hear a sermon doesn't ask much of you. It certainly will never expose you. That's why most folks prefer it. Because community will. It will reveal where you have yet to become holy, right at the very moment you are so keenly aware of how *they* have yet to become holy. It will bring you close and you will be *seen* and you will be *known,* and therein lies the power and therein lies the danger. Aren't there moments when all those little companies, in all those stories, hang by a thread? Galadriel says to Frodo, "Your quest stands upon the edge of a knife. Stray but a little and it will fail, to the ruin of all. Yet hope remains while the Company is true."

We've experienced incredible disappointments in our fellowship. We have, every last one of us, hurt one another. Sometimes deeply. Last year there was a night when Stasi and I laid out a vision for where we thought things should be going—our lifelong dream for redemptive community. We hoped the Company would leap to it with loud hurrahs. "Hurrah for John and Stasi!" Far from it. Their response was more on the level of blank stares. Our dream was mishandled—badly. Stasi was sick to her stomach; she wanted to leave the room and throw up. I was . . . stunned. Disappointed. I felt the dive toward a total loss of heart. The following day I could feel my heart being pulled toward resentment. Moments like that usually toll the beginning of the end for most attempts at community.

Seriously now—how often have you seen this sort of intimate community work? It is *rare*. Because it is hard, and it is fiercely *opposed*. The Enemy hates this sort of thing; he knows how powerful it can be, for God and his kingdom. For our hearts. It is devastating to him. Remember divide and conquer? Most churches survive because everyone keeps a polite distance from the others. We keep our meetings short, our conversations superficial. "So, Ted, how's everything going on the Stewardship Committee?" "Oh, just great, Nancy. We've got a big goal to reach this year, but I think we'll be able to get that gym after all." No one is really being set free, but no one is really at odds with each other, either. We have settled for safety in numbers—a comfortable, anonymous distance. An army that keeps meeting for briefings, but never breaks into platoons and goes to war.

Living in community is like camping together. For a month. In the desert. Without tents. All your stuff is scattered out there for everyone to see. C'mon—anybody can look captured for Christ an hour a week, from a distance, in his Sunday best. But your life is open to those you live in community with. Some philosopher described it like a pack of porcupines on a winter night. You come together because of the cold, and you are forced apart because of the spines. *Here we go again. Why does Jim always have to be discouraged? I'm sick of encouraging him. And what is it with Mary and her inability to stop talking about herself? Why is Brian always so guarded? These people* bug *me.*

However, there are two things you now have that you didn't have before, and they enable this sort of fellowship to work. First, you know the heart is good. That is the missing key in most fellowships. Your heart is good, and the others' hearts are good. This makes it so much easier to trust and to forgive. Whatever may be happening in the moment, whatever the misunderstanding might be, I know that our hearts toward one another are good, and that we are for one another. Craig says something that stings. If I thought, *You know, he meant that; he's trying to hurt me,* it would pretty quickly trash the relationship. But I know that is not his heart toward me; that is not who he truly is. If I thought it was, why, I'd turn tail and run.

Second, we know we are at war. The thought that says, *Oh, brother, here goes Frank again. Why can't he just drop it about his mother? What is it with these people? They're not really my friends. I'm outta here.* That's the Enemy. You *must* remember that the Enemy is always trying to pull everyone else to do to you what *he* is doing to you. As I said earlier, he creates a kind of force field, a gravitational pull around you that draws others into the plot without their even knowing it. Gary walks into the room and, suddenly, I'm irritated at him. It's not me, and it's not him. I have to know that. His lifelong assault has been, "If you can't get it right, we don't want to be with you." It's a lie. It's the Enemy. I don't feel that way toward him *really.* But unless I live with this awareness, keep a watchful eye out for it, and resist, I'll get sucked into the pull, start making agreements with it, and there goes the friendship.

FIGHT FOR IT

> Be kind, for everyone you know is facing a great battle. (Philo of Alexandria)

A true community is something you'll have to fight for. You'll have to fight to get one, and you'll have to fight to keep it afloat. But you fight for it as you bail out a life raft during a storm at sea. You want this thing to work. You *need* this thing to work. You can't ditch it and jump back on the cruise ship. This *is* the church; this is all you have. Without it, you'll go down. Or back to captivity. This is the reason those small house fellowships thrive in other countries: they *need* each other. There are no other options.

Suddenly, all those *one another*'s in Scripture make sense. Love one another. Bear one another's burdens. Forgive one another. Acts of kindness become deeply meaningful because we know we are at war. Knowing full well that we all are facing battles of our own, we give one another the benefit of the doubt. *Leigh isn't intentionally being distant from me—she's probably under an assault.* That's why you must know each other's stories, know how to "read" each other. A word of encouragement can heal a wound; a choice to forgive can destroy a stronghold. You never knew your simple acts were so *weighty*. It's what we've come to call "lifestyle warfare."

We check in regularly with one another, not out of paranoia ("Do you still like me?"), but out of a desire to watch over one another's hearts. "How are you doing?" But be careful about what you are looking for from community. For if you bring your every need to it, it will collapse. Community is no substitute for God. I left our annual camping trip absolutely exhausted and disappointed. As we drove home, I realized I was looking to them to validate me, appreciate me, fill this aching void in my heart. Only once in ten days did I take time to be away with God, alone. I was too busy trying to get my needs met through them. Which is why community cannot live without solitude.

I was so struck by the layout of the early Irish and Scottish monasteries when we visited there last year. First, they knew they *had* to live in community. They needed each other. But in every single location, set apart from the community buildings by about a twenty-minute walk, you'd find little "cells," small stone huts designed for one member to get alone and be with God. They knew community could not survive without solitude. There is a rhythm to life together, as Bonhoeffer said. We first go to God, alone, so that we have something to bring back to the community. This is part of lifestyle warfare. I know my community needs me; everyone is coming over tonight. So I'd better get with God this afternoon. I want to contribute. I want to play a vital role.

The Time Has Come Again

It's the little platoons that change the world. This has always been true.

In 564 Saint Columba (Columcille in Gaelic) left his beloved Ireland in a coracle, sail unfurled, willing to let God lead him wherever he might for the sake of the gospel. With him were twelve disciples, friends, warrior-monks as they would later be called. They landed on a small island off the coast of Scotland (at the time a dark, vicious, pagan country), and there they established what they called a "little heavenly community." The place was Iona, and it became the center of a new and vibrant Christianity.

Now, in order to realize what Iona was and what it means for us, you must understand the context of that moment in history. First, the world around them had grown very dark. Night had fallen with the fall of Rome; the Vandals and the Goths and the Visigoths and all those predatory gangs had swept down upon Europe and basically ransacked the place. Western Europe was like L.A. during the riots. Paganism flourished; law and order were long gone. It was barbarous.

But you must also know that at the time of Iona, the Christian church based in Rome was already becoming institutionalized, hierarchical, far more an organization than it was an organism. That living and spontaneous association of individuals who know one another intimately and care for one another deeply was giving way to a large, centralized, bureaucratic church where rules and bylaws become necessary. Sad, but true. And so I hope you see that it was a time very much like our own. A world, come to think of it, very much like the one the early church also found itself in. The synagogue was dead, and the cultures around them pagan indeed. What did they do? They came together into little fellowships of the heart.

Iona and its warrior-monks began to carry their light into that darkness. Columba won to Christ the king of the Picts, the notorious pagan warriors of northern Scotland who painted their faces blue before battle (the precursors of *Braveheart*). In winning him, Columba won over a great deal of Scotland. Iona also became the staging point for missionary raids into England and deep into Europe. In this way, Irish monasticism and Celtic Christianity began to change the world. Everywhere they went, they established communities like their own, little "fellowships of the heart" along the way. It was the book of Acts all over again. It was a spirituality of the heart, based in a community that knew it was at war, and it was unstoppable. Historian Thomas Cahill said Iona "forever changed the course of western history."

> Celtic spirituality is not a top-down form of church, but bottom-up. It allows spirituality to flow from the heart. It allows the five senses to be used. It's creative. It's a flowering of creative arts. It's an expression of Christianity which believes that to be Christian is to be fully human. (Ray Simpson, Lindisfarne Community)

They believed that the glory of God is man fully alive.

Our trip to Iona last year was a sort of pilgrimage, and I can tell you, it is still a remarkable place. The veil between the worlds is very thin there. As we strolled among the ruins, read their accounts, looked at their way of life, I realized that this was not the faith of some good people applying biblical principles to their lives in a fairly benign, though disappointing and fallen world. Here was the burning-heart conviction of a group of increasingly glorious men and women who wanted the freedom and life and restoration Christ promised, and who were willing to fight for it because they

knew this is a world at war. A community of people living in the
Four Streams because they knew the Christian life as an *epic,* no less
than the greatest myths the world has ever known.

We paused by one of the ancient Celtic crosses. God spoke, and
this is what he said:

I am doing this again.

God is calling together little communities of the heart, to fight
for one another and for the hearts of those who have not yet been
set free. That camaraderie, that intimacy, that incredible impact by
a few stouthearted souls—that is available. It is the Christian life as
Jesus gave it to us. It is completely normal.

CHAPTER TWELVE

LIKE THE TREASURES
OF THE KINGDOM

Arise, shine, for your light has come,
   and the glory of the LORD rises upon you.
See, darkness covers the earth
   and thick darkness is over the peoples,
but the LORD rises upon you
   and his glory appears over you.

                —ISAIAH (60:1–2)

And then my soul, awaking with the morn
Shall be a waking joy, eternally new-born.

                —GEORGE MACDONALD

Jesus, once more deeply moved, came to the tomb. It was a cave with a stone laid across the entrance. "Take away the stone," he said. "But, Lord," said Martha, the sister of the dead man, "by this time there is a bad odor, for he has been there four days." Then Jesus said, "Did I not tell you that if you believed, you would see the glory of God?" So they took away the stone. Then Jesus looked up and said, "Father, I thank you that you have heard me. I knew that you always hear me, but I said this for the benefit of the people standing here, that they may believe that you sent me." When he had said this, Jesus called in a loud voice, "Lazarus, come out!" The dead man came out, his hands and feet wrapped with strips of linen, and a cloth around his face. Jesus said to them, "Take off the grave clothes and let him go." (John 11:38–44)

And when Jesus had cried out again in a loud voice, he gave up his spirit. At that moment the curtain of the temple was torn in two from top to bottom. The earth shook and the rocks split. The tombs broke open and the bodies of many holy people who had died were raised to life. They came out of the tombs, and after Jesus' resurrection they went into the holy city and appeared to many people. (Matt. 27:50–53)

ARISE

I awoke in the desert on Easter morning.

Through the window of my tent, I could see branches of a pinion pine, the sharp tines of a yucca, and beyond them soft, rolling sandstone—in full daylight the color of oatmeal, but glowing golden now with first light. The birds were up, rejoicing, flitting to and fro in the pinion, but, thanks be to God, not another living thing could be seen or heard. I had awakened on my fifth morning in Arches National Park, hidden near the northeast corner of Utah, but it could have been Palestine around A.D. 33. This desert is not a wasteland, as many people wrongly picture when they hear the word, but a vibrant place full of grasses, cacti, juniper and pinion, and wildflowers scattered across the landscape, a place where you can find puma prints in the soft, wet sand down in the canyons, where springs nearly reach the surface. A place of life in many ways.

It was cold enough to see my breath when I stepped out of the tent, so I cranked the Coleman stove to set water boiling for coffee and cocoa before I roused the boys, cocooned head-and-all down in their sleeping bags. Savoring moments that were mine alone, I climbed to the top of the rocks behind our camp, to drink in the vast beauty of the desert at dawn. To the west, gigantic mesas, Navajo sandstone, rose like ancient fortresses from the desert floor, their sheer red cliffs radiating back the rays that had not reached the sands at their feet.

I turned to the east to take the glad warmth of the new day head-on, surprised to see the La Sal Mountains covered in snow, a hundred miles away. My heart was at home in this place of wild beauty and staggering vistas. But it was an awkward time to have come. On this resurrection morn, Stasi was in Los Angeles, holding the hand of her dying mother. She would be gone in less than a month. Strange timing to up and go camping. But God brought me here.

Like many pilgrims down through the ages, I discovered my spiritual life in the desert. I found solitude and silence in the Mojave of southern California, far from the numbing sameness and suffocating density of the suburbs that warehouse millions of people. The desert awakened my heart, and I discovered freedom of spirit walking across the arroyos for hours upon end, haunted by stark beauty and the thin veil of heaven there. No wonder Moses, Elijah, and John the Baptist spent their free time in the desert. And though the desert meant so much to me, spoke to my heart, I left it behind many years ago. You know how life pickpockets you of these things, slipping them away so subtly you never even notice they are gone. I simply stopped going.

In the spring of 2001, Stasi was making frequent trips to southern California to be with her mom, whom we were losing to multiple myeloma, and I was doing my best with the boys and the bills back home in Colorado. To be honest, we were simply waiting for "the call," when we would jump a flight to attend Jane's funeral. So I did not believe it was God when first I heard him say, *Go to Moab. Go to the desert.* It took several confirmations to get my attention. At a coffeehouse I ran into a young gal who in the midst of chitchat simply dropped into the conversation that she'd just returned from Moab. I did a sort of double take, then asked calmly, "How was it?" "Great," she said. "You have to go." The next day I was on the phone with a pastor from Denver, making plans for a men's retreat. "I just got back from Moab," he said, out of the blue. "It was awesome." I'm simply confessing that I came to the desert borne not on the wings of my own wisdom, but hesitantly, reluctantly, pushed along by God.

Moab. Okay. The boys are missing Mom and the distraction would be good and there's really nothing more we can do from here anyway except pray, which I might give more devotion to out in the wild, and so we came. I was surprised at the level of warfare I had to fight through. For about five hours of the drive I was forced to bring the work of Christ against an overwhelming oppression that made it hard to concentrate, a really awful veil over my spirit. Over a *camping* trip? It seemed so stupid. But the thief comes to steal and kill and destroy *any* movement toward freedom and life. We battled through, got there late, and discovered that God had held the last campsite for us.

I'm not sure I can even put into words all that Jesus restored to me in those five days, but some part of my heart long forgotten was given back, along with some deep words I desperately needed. I came alive in the vast, wild desert. And it began to sink in. *My heart matters to God. My heart has always mattered to him.* It is one thing to say we believe that; it is another thing to *discover* it is true. This was a gift unique to my heart, and it could not have been given in any other place. I awoke that Easter morning more alive than I have been in a long, long time.

TREATING YOUR HEART FOR THE TREASURE IT IS

"Above all else, guard your heart" (Prov. 4:23). We usually hear this with a sense of "keep an eye on that heart of yours," in the way you'd warn a deputy watching over some dangerous outlaw, or a bad dog the neighbors let run. "Don't let him out of your sight." Having so long believed our hearts are evil, we assume the warning is to keep us out of trouble. So we lock up our hearts and throw away the key, and then try to get on with our living. But that isn't the spirit of the command at all. It doesn't say guard your heart because it's criminal; it says guard your heart because it is the well-spring of your life, because it is a *treasure,* because everything else depends on it. How kind of God to give us this warning, like some-one's entrusting to a friend something precious to him, with the words: "Be careful with this—it means a lot to me."

Above all else? Good grief—we don't even do it once in a while. We might as well leave our life savings on the seat of the car with the windows rolled down—we're that careless with our hearts. "If not for my careless heart," sang Roy Orbison, and it might be the anthem for our lives. Things would be different. I would be farther along. My faith would be much deeper. My relationships so much better. My life would be on the path God meant for me . . . if not for my careless heart. We live completely backward. "All else" is above our hearts. I'll wager that caring for your heart isn't even a category you think in. "Let's see—I've got to get the kids to soccer, the car needs to be dropped off at the shop, and I need to take a couple of hours for *my* heart this week." It probably sounds unbib-lical, even after all we've covered.

Seriously now—what do you do on a daily basis to care for your heart? Okay, that wasn't fair. How about weekly? *Monthly?*

Yes, we do have a cultural scrap of this called vacation. Most working-class folks get a week or two off each year, and that is the only time they actually plan to do something that might be good for their souls. Or they squander the scrap on some place like Miami, as a poor man spends his last dollar on a lottery ticket. And you know how it goes when you get back. The attitude among your family, friends, and colleagues is usually something like, "Great! You're back! Hope you had a good time 'cause, boy, everything fell apart while you were gone and we're expecting—now that you're rested up—that you'll really put your nose to the grindstone." Whatever that week gave you is devoured in a matter of moments or days.

But God intends that we treat our hearts as the treasures of the kingdom, ransomed at tremendous cost, as if they really *do* matter, and matter deeply.

STORING UP TO OVERFLOW

> If then you are wise, you will show yourself rather as a reservoir than as a canal. A canal spreads abroad water as it receives it, but a reservoir waits until it is filled before overflowing, and thus without loss to itself [it shares] its superabundant water. (Bernard of Clairvaux)

A beautiful picture. The canal runs dry so quickly, shortly after the rains subside. Like a dry streambed in the desert. But a reservoir is a vast and deep reserve of life. We are called to live in a way that we store up reserves in our hearts and *then* offer from a place of abundance. Jesus said, "Every teacher of the law who has been instructed about the kingdom of heaven is like the owner of a house who brings out of his storeroom new treasures as well as old" (Matt. 13:52). I'm thinking, *Storeroom? What storeroom?* "The good man brings good things out of the good stored up *in his heart* . . . For out of the overflow of his heart his mouth speaks" (Luke 6:45, emphasis added).

I'm afraid I live spiritually the same way I live financially—I get a little and go spend it. I live like a canal. I *look* like a reservoir when the rains come, but shortly after, I'm dried up again. (My financially responsible readers have just congratulated themselves on living a more disciplined life. But may I ask, Are you using those reserves to do things that nourish your heart? Many a Scrooge has filled his coffers while starving his soul.) "There are very many canals in the church today," laments Julia Gatta, "but few reservoirs." One woman deeply involved in ministry wrote to me recently that she is "burned out to a crackling crunch." She has been a canal. She hasn't cared for her heart. She is not alone.

How would you live differently if you believed your heart was the treasure of the kingdom?

This is what God tells us to do, above all else, as the passage says. Last week over breakfast I asked a small group of friends—men who fight for the hearts of others all the time—"What are you doing these days to care for your heart?" They fell silent, eyes roaming the floor, staring at their eggs, examining their nails as if they were pondering a really good answer, but nothing ever came. I was saddened, but not surprised. Our hearts are always the first things to go.

But did you know that God gives out of the *abundance* of his heart? One of the first things John tells us about his dear friend Jesus is that "from the fullness of his grace we have all received one blessing after another" (John 1:16). From God's *fullness,* we receive blessing. Or as Paul prays in Ephesians, "I pray that out of his glorious riches he may strengthen you" (3:16), which is to say, out of the riches God has stored up in his great heart, he gives to ours. Dallas Willard reminds us,

> He is full of joy. Undoubtedly he is the most joyous being in the universe. The abundance of his love and generosity is inseparable from his infinite joy. All of the good and beautiful things from which we occasionally drink [Willard includes the sea in all its beauty, or a wonderful movie, or music] . . . God continuously experiences in all their breadth and depth and richness.

Has it ever occurred to you that God is such a loving and generous person *because* his heart is filled, like a reservoir, with joy? It is because his heart is brimming with good things and experiences that God is able to love and forgive and suffer so long for mankind. The same holds true for us. Are you a delight to be with after an hour in traffic? No wonder we are so short on grace and mercy. Life drains us dry—and we just accept it as the normal way to live.

We were really burned out, Stasi and I, when we headed off to this year's annual family vacation. Before we left, she told me she was "done with people." I was too. Even a short conversation felt draining. Neither of us wanted to see anyone. We gave some serious thought to becoming hermits. Enough of this community stuff. Living alone in a hut in the Kalahari sounded like paradise. God's remedy was eight days in southeast Alaska, photographing grizzly bears, sea kayaking with humpback whales, eating more than our share of great food, and drinking in breathtaking views in every direction. We got home late on a Saturday night; I woke Sunday morning to hear Stasi chatting away on the phone with a friend. She called another and another all day long. "Just catching up," she said with a smile.

As an Act of Love

Caring for our own hearts isn't selfishness; it's how we begin to love.

Yes, we care for our hearts for the sake of others. Does that sound like a contradiction? Not at all. What will you bring to others if your heart is empty, dried up, pinned down? Love is the point. And you can't love without your heart, and you can't love well unless your heart is well.

When it comes to the whole subject of loving others, you must know this: how you handle your own heart is how you will handle theirs. This is the wisdom behind Jesus' urging us to love others *as we love ourselves* (Mark 12:31). "A horrible command," as C. S. Lewis points out, "if the self were simply to be hated." If you dismiss your heart, you will end up dismissing theirs. If you expect perfection of your heart, you will raise that same standard for them. If you manage your heart for efficiency and performance, that is what you'll pressure them to be.

"But," you protest, "I have lots of grace for other people. I'm just hard on myself." I tried the same excuse for years. It doesn't work. Even though we may try to be merciful toward others while we neglect or beat up ourselves, they can *see* how we treat our own hearts, and they will always feel the treatment will be the same for them. They are right. Eventually, inevitably, we will treat them poorly too.

You know this without knowing that you did. There are certain people you would never go to with a problem, would never call at 2:00 A.M. when you were struggling under some burden or loss. Why not? You know they would not handle your heart well. Some folks I know won some airline tickets good for travel to anyplace in the world. That was fifteen years ago. They still haven't used them. Would you ask them for advice on caring for your heart? Don't you sense they would say, "There's no time for that"?

Yes, there is a place for sacrifice. And yes, I know, a lot of very selfish things have been done under the excuse that "I'm taking care of my heart." I've heard divorces and affairs justified that way. But the fact that someone abuses an idea doesn't make it a bad idea. People overeat too. Does that mean you shouldn't enjoy eating? Some pretty awful things have been done in the name of Christianity. Does that mean you shouldn't be a Christian? Don't let others' bad choices shape your life. Care for your heart. Above all else. Not only for your own sake; not even primarily for your own sake. Do it in order to love better, for the sake of those who need you. And they need you. Remember—this is our most desperate hour.

AS AN ACT OF DEVOTION

Caring for your heart is also how you protect your relationship with God.

Now there's a new thought. But isn't our heart the new dwelling place of God? It is where we commune with him. It is where we hear his voice. Most of the folks I know who have never heard God speak to them are the same folks who live far from their hearts; they practice the Christianity of principles. Then they wonder why God seems distant. *I guess all that intimacy with God stuff is for others, not me.* It's like a friend who hates the telephone. He neglects to pay the bills, could care less when the phone company disconnects the service. Then he wonders why "nobody ever calls." You cannot cut off your heart and expect to hear from God.

The same holds true for those folks who cannot seem to find the abundant life that Christ promised. Your heart is where that life flows into you. "On the last and greatest day of the Feast, Jesus stood and said in a loud voice, 'If anyone is thirsty, let him come to me and drink. Whoever believes in me, as the Scripture has said, streams of living water will flow from within him'" (John 7:37–38). "Flow from within" means "from your inmost being," from your heart, that wellspring of life within you. God *wants* to give you his life; your part is to keep the channel open. You do that by caring for your heart.

Clairvaux describes Christian maturity as the stage where "we love ourselves for God's sake," meaning that because he considers our hearts the treasures of the kingdom, we do too. We care for ourselves in the same way a woman who knows she is deeply loved cares for herself, while a woman who has been tossed aside tends to "let herself go," as the saying goes. God's friends care for their hearts because they matter to *him*.

What Will You Do?

So, let me ask again: How would you live differently if you believed your heart was the treasure of the kingdom?

What does your heart need? In some sense it's a personal question, unique to our makeup and what brings us life. For some it's music; for others it's reading; for still others it's gardening. Our friend Lori loves the city; I can't wait to get out of one. Bart reads articles on flying; Cherie loves a good novel. Bethann loves horses, and Gary needs time working in the woodshop. You know what makes your heart refreshed, the things that make you come alive. I don't get the thing with women and baths, but I know that Stasi loves them and finds a little retreat in a fifteen-minute tub: "He leads me to soak in bubbly waters." For me and the boys it's the dirtier, the happier.

Yet there are some needs that all hearts have in common. We need beauty; that's clear enough from the fact that God has filled the world with it. He has given us sun and rain,

> wine that gladdens the heart of man,
>> oil to make his face shine,
>> and bread that sustains his heart. (Ps. 104:15)

We need to drink in beauty wherever we can get it—in music, in nature, in art, in a great meal shared. These are all gifts to us from God's generous heart. Friends, those things are not decorations to a life; they bring us life.

> The skies of blue
> The fields of green
> Are all for you
>
> The silver moon
> The shining sea

All for you

For you, the wind blows
For you, the river flows

And everything you dream about
Even the love you dream of, too,
Is all for you. (John Smith and Lisa Aschmann, "All for You")

I don't think I could have finished this book if it weren't for the walks I take each day in the woods. Last night it began to snow. It is still snowing now. It, too, is a gift to my heart. Early this morning I just sat and watched it fall; so quiet and beautiful, it felt like a balm to my soul.

We need silence and solitude. Often. Jesus modeled that, though few of us ever follow his example. Not even one full chapter into the gospel of Mark, there's quite a stir being created by the Nazarene. "The whole town gathered at the door," which is to say, Jesus is becoming the man to see. Let's pick up the story there:

> That evening after sunset the people brought to Jesus all the sick and demon-possessed. The whole town gathered at the door, and Jesus healed many who had various diseases . . . Very early in the morning, while it was still dark, Jesus got up, left the house and went off to a solitary place, where he prayed. Simon and his companions went to look for him, and when they found him, they exclaimed: "Everyone is looking for you!" Jesus replied, "Let us go somewhere else." (1:32–38)

"Everyone is looking for you!" Surely you can relate to that. At work, at home, at church, aren't there times when everything seems to come down on you? Now this is a tremendous opportunity. I mean, if Jesus really wants to launch his ministry, increase sales, expand his audience, this sure looks like the chance to do it. What does he do? He leaves. He walks away. Everyone is looking for you! Oh, really . . . then we'd better leave. It cracks me up. Wendell Berry might have been writing of Jesus when he said, "His wildness was in his refusal—or his inability—to live within other people's expectations." We are just the opposite; our entire lives are ruled by the expectations of others, and when we live like that, the heart is always the first thing to go.

Let me ask again: What does *your* heart need? A simple starting place would be to ask God: *What do you have for my heart?* You'll be stunned by what he guides you into.

My parents recently came for a visit. It was a good time, but it fell during a lot of other demands on me, and by the time the week was over, I was wiped out physically, emotionally, spiritually. I hadn't had a moment to myself. As I was driving them to the airport, my dad mentioned that he'd read in the local sports section that the fishing had been good up at one of my old favorite spots. I passed it over with a "huh." On the way home, God whispered, *Go fishing.* What? I haven't time to do that. It was the last thing on my mind. *Take your canoe, call Morgan, and go to the lake.* Now, you need to understand my reluctance. For one thing, the canoe was serving as a storage bin for every piece of flotsam and jetsam in my garage. It was buried. For another, I hadn't been to that lake in four years . . . not since the day my best friend died.

But I've learned to trust God on these urgings, and so I called my buddy, dug out the canoe, found my gear, and went. It was a gorgeous scene. The waters were completely calm, like glass, and there wasn't another soul around. We pushed out, and within a few minutes we were catching these enormous rainbows, one after another, laughing and whooping and having a ball. I'm a little embarrassed to admit it, but I was stunned. Simply stunned. *Really, God? My heart matters to you?*

You might not think God wants this for you . . . but have you asked him? I think I've missed thousands of little promptings over the years, simply because I wasn't open to the fact that they occur. But I am astounded and more than humbled by the number of gifts he has given my heart since I've begun to give even partial heed to Proverbs 4:23. And I know I'm not some special case. Just this week, on Tuesday night, the people in our home fellowship were reviewing some notes from an exercise we'd done together at the first of the year. We'd taken an evening to write down the things we'd love to see happen in our lives in the coming year. It's a simple way of listening to what your heart needs: What do you want? What is your heart longing for?

Ten months had passed when Jenny suggested we have a look at what we'd jotted down. Reviewing our desires was astounding in two ways. First, most of us had completely forgotten what we were longing for. (The sign of an abandoned heart: we didn't even remember our own dreams.) Stasi hadn't recalled wanting to speak to women. I'd forgotten that I wanted to go to Alaska. Leigh had forgotten wanting to dance. Joni had forgotten her desire to visit the Tetons. But what was even more astounding was that *God* had not forgotten. We'd gone to Alaska. Joni had gone to the Tetons. Leigh had danced—and beautifully. Stasi spoke at her first women's retreat—and gloriously. On every single person's list—in more cases than not—God had given us our heart's desire. Wow. Our hearts *do* matter to God.

Now, the Enemy will tell you this is foolish. *There are so many more important things to do. You can get to it some other time. You're being selfish. This isn't even what you want, anyway.* Remember: he fears you—fears your heart's coming alive and full and free. Caring for your heart is an act of obedience. It is an act of love, an act of faith, an act of war.

AS AN ACT OF WAR

Caring for your heart is your first blow against the Enemy's schemes.

The heart that is weak is vulnerable. Are you able to fend off accusation when you are wiped out from a hard week? It seems so true at that point, and who really cares anyway? You know how draining the holidays can be. Are you overflowing with prayer the day after Christmas? Listen—the first wave of any strike against us is to rob us of the heart to fight it. It always starts that way, with that sense of being too tired or overwhelmed. Heads up—the main assault is coming on the heels of it. Facing an overwhelming enemy at Agincourt, King Henry prays for his men, that the opposing numbers will not "pluck their hearts from them."

It works like this: hyenas cannot bring down a lion in its prime. What they do is run it and taunt it and wear it down to the point of exhaustion. Once they see it cannot defend itself, then they close in. The strategy of our Enemy in the age we live in now is *busyness* or *drivenness*. Ask the people you know how things are going. Nine out of ten will answer something to the effect of "really busy." Every time I call another ministry I get voice mail. "They're busy right now, can I put you into voice mail?" The deadly scheme is this: *keep them running. That way, they'll never take care of their hearts. We'll burn them out and take them out.*

I don't want to be taken out. Others are counting on me. I must care for my heart as my first line of defense.

Also, an empty heart is more vulnerable to temptation. Isn't it when you're sad and discouraged that a bag of donuts looks like salvation? When you're bored and lonely that the adult cable channel seems irresistible? A heart that has been cared for is like a man or woman deeply in love—an affair isn't even appealing when you have the real deal. It's the famished heart that falls for seduction. There's a great picture of this in the film *Chocolat*. The mayor of the town is a Pharisee, a legalist bound to rules. He denies his heart, hates it, fears it. He goes in one night to destroy the chocolate shop and ends up binging himself into a coma, his starving heart taken out by some fudge.

Be kind to yourself. Take care of your heart. You're going to need it.

AND WE ARE AT WAR, DEAR FRIENDS

If you have raced with men on foot
    and they have worn you out,
      how can you compete with horses?
If you stumble in safe country,
      how will you manage in the thickets by the Jordan? (Jer. 12:5)

Look—it's going to get worse before it gets better. Jesus warned us about that. So let me say, one more time, *we are at war*. The worst scenes in *The Lord of the Rings* or *The Matrix* or *Gladiator* are merely trying to wake you to the reality in which you now live. The Ransom of your life commands you to *take care of your heart . . . now*. He knows what's coming.

Something like the battle for Iwo Jima is coming—spiritually, in our own lives, and in the life of the body of Christ around the world. To say it was one of the bloodiest, ugliest, most heroic battles in the history of war is true, but hardly captures it. John Wayne's movie doesn't even come close to what really happened there. It was . . . horrifying beyond words. Picture the opening scenes from *Saving Private Ryan,* and multiply them by a factor of three. The Japanese had studied the Allied victory at Normandy to prepare against this invasion. They transformed the little island, a tiny scrap of rock out in the Pacific, into a fortress maze of tunnels, bunkers, pillboxes, and underground caverns to conceal 22,000 Japanese soldiers who had, like crazed kamikazes, pledged themselves to die defending the island.

The young marines who landed on Iwo Jima were forced to drive out the Japanese inch by inch, battling an enemy they could not see while being exposed to every sort of weapons fire from every possible direction. Mortars, machine guns, mines, grenades. Some survivors reported that they never saw one living Japanese soldier in all those days of combat. (Sounds just like spiritual warfare.) Military analysts thought the battle could be won in seventy-two hours. It took thirty-six days and cost nearly seven thousand American lives. More medals of honor were awarded for action there than in any other battle in U.S. history. On the second day of the invasion, one war reporter, leaving the field, warned a colleague, "I wouldn't go in there if I were you. There's more hell in there than I've seen in the rest of the war put together."

The men of Easy Company were among the first to descend into that hell, and among the last to pull out after fighting more than five straight weeks. Their unit suffered 85 percent casualties. Easy landed on the far left end of Green Beach One, the end of the line. They led the assault on Mount Suribachi. Two thousand entrenched Japanese began firing everything they had at the totally exposed marines. Not just for hours or days, but *weeks*. On the fifteenth day of battle, Easy was pulled off the front line for a breather. Their captain removed the company to a secured beach on the west side of the island. Their orders?

Take a swim.

TAKE HEART

We now are going to war. This is the beginning of the end. The hour is late, and you are needed. We need your heart.

If there were something more I could do to help you see, I wish to God I could have done it. Tears fill my eyes for fear I have not done enough. You must turn, then, back to myth—tomorrow and the next day and the next. Read the battle of Helm's Deep; it's chapter 7 of *The Two Towers*. Watch any of the trilogy of those films. And the opening of *Gladiator*. That is where we are now. Or if you can bear it, watch the battle of the Ia Drang Valley in *We Were Soldiers*. It is so deeply true to what we must face, will face. Linger over the climax of *The Prince of Egypt*, where God goes to war against Egypt to set his people free. If the images of the Exodus do not move you, I don't know what will.

Read Lewis's last installment in *The Chronicles of Narnia*, titled *The Last Battle*. I don't think even he knew all he was saying there. These stories and images are among the stories that God is giving to his people for this hour. They are gifts to us from his hand, clarity and strength for our hearts. Apparently, we need them. They will do you a great good. And then . . . you will do a great good. Remember our friends from the Emmaus Road? Well, the story ends with their eyes wide open. They go tearing back to Jerusalem, their hearts bursting. "They found the Eleven and those with them, assembled together and saying, 'It is true!'" (Luke 24:33–34). It is true. All of it.

We are now far into this epic Story that every great myth points to. We have reached the moment where we, too, must find our courage and rise up to recover our hearts and fight for the hearts of others. The hour is late, and much time has been wasted. Aslan is on the move; we must rally to him at the stone table. We must find Gepetto lost at sea. We must ride hard, ride to Helm's Deep and join the last great battle for Middle Earth. Grab everything God sends you. You'll need everything that helps you see with the eyes of your heart, including those myths, and the way they illumine for us the words God has given in Scripture, to which "you will do well to pay attention . . . as to a light shining in a dark place, until the day dawns and the morning star rises in your hearts" (2 Peter 1:19).

Yes. Until the day dawns, my friends, and the Morning Star rises in all our *hearts*.

Wake up, O sleeper,
rise from the dead,
and Christ will shine on you.
—THE APOSTLE PAUL
(Eph. 5:14)

A Daily Prayer
for Freedom

My dear Lord Jesus, I come to you now to be restored in you—to renew my place in you, my allegiance to you, and to receive from you all the grace and mercy I so desperately need this day. I honor you as my sovereign Lord, and I surrender every aspect of my life totally and completely to you. I give you my body as a living sacrifice; I give you my heart, soul, mind, and strength; and I give you my spirit as well.

I cover myself with your blood—my spirit, my soul, and my body. And I ask your Holy Spirit to restore my union with you, seal me in you, and guide me in this time of prayer. In all that I now pray, I include (my wife, and/or my children, by name). Acting as their head, I bring them under my authority and covering, and I come under your authority and covering. Holy Spirit, apply to them all that I now pray on their behalf.

Dear God, holy and victorious Trinity, you alone are worthy of all my worship, my heart's devotion, all my praise and all my trust and all the glory of my life. I worship you, bow to you, and give myself over to you in my heart's search for life. You alone are Life, and you have become my life. I renounce all other gods, all idols, and I give you the place in my heart and in my life that you truly deserve. I confess here and now that it is all about you, God, and not about me. You are the Hero of this story, and I belong to you. Forgive me, God, for my every sin. Search me and know me and reveal to me any aspect of my life that is not pleasing to you, expose any agreements I have made, and grant me the grace of a deep and true repentance.

Heavenly Father, thank you for loving me and choosing me before you made the world. You are my true Father—my Creator, my Redeemer, my Sustainer, and the true end of all things, including my life. I love you; I trust you; I worship you. Thank you for proving your love for me by sending your only Son, Jesus, to be my substitute and representative. I receive him and all his life and all his work, which you ordained for me. Thank you for including me in Christ, for forgiving me my sins, for granting me his righteousness, for making me complete in him. Thank you for making me alive with Christ, raising me with him, seating me with him at your right hand, granting me his authority, and anointing me with your Holy Spirit. I receive it all with thanks and give it total claim to my life.

Jesus, thank you for coming for me, for ransoming me with your own life. I honor you as my Lord; I love you, worship you, trust you. I sincerely receive you as my redemption, and I receive all the work and triumph of your crucifixion, whereby I am cleansed from all my sin through your shed blood, my old nature is removed, my heart is circumcised unto God, and every claim being made against me is disarmed. I take my place in your cross and death, whereby I have died with you to sin and to my flesh, to the world, and to the Evil One. I am crucified with Christ, and I have crucified my flesh with all its passions and desires. I take up my cross and crucify my flesh with all its pride, unbelief, and idolatry. I put off the old man. I now bring the cross of Christ between me and all people, all spirits, all things. Holy Spirit, apply to me (my wife and/or children) the fullness of the work of the crucifixion of Jesus Christ for me. I receive it with thanks and give it total claim to my life.

Jesus, I also sincerely receive you as my new life, my holiness and sanctification, and I receive all the work and triumph of your resurrection, whereby I have been raised with you to a new life, to walk in newness of life, dead to sin and alive to God. I am crucified with Christ, and it is no longer I who live but Christ who lives in me. I now take my place in your resurrection, whereby I have been made alive with you, I reign in life through you. I now put on the new man in all holiness and humility, in all righteousness and purity and truth. Christ is now my life, the one who strengthens me. Holy Spirit, apply to me (my wife and/or my children) the fullness of the resurrection of Jesus Christ for me. I receive it with thanks and give it total claim to my life.

Jesus, I also sincerely receive you as my authority and rule, my everlasting victory over Satan and his kingdom, and I receive all the work and triumph of your ascension, whereby Satan has been judged and cast down, his rulers and authorities disarmed, all authority in heaven and on earth given to you, Jesus, and I have been given fullness in you, the Head over all. I take my place in your ascension, whereby I have been raised with you to the right hand of the Father and established with you in all authority. I bring your authority and your kingdom rule over my life, my family, my household, and my domain.

And now I bring the fullness of your work—your cross, resurrection, and ascension—against Satan, against his kingdom, and against all his emissaries and all their work warring against me and my domain. Greater is he who is in me than he who is in the world. Christ has given me authority to overcome all the power of the Evil One, and I claim that authority now over and against every enemy, and I banish them in the name of Jesus Christ. Holy Spirit, apply to me (my wife and my children) the fullness of the work of the ascension of Jesus Christ for me. I receive it with thanks and give it total claim to my life.

Holy Spirit, I sincerely receive you as my Counselor, my Comforter, my Strength, and my Guide. Thank you for sealing me in Christ. I honor you as my Lord, and I ask you to lead me into all truth, to anoint me for all of my life and walk and calling, and to lead me deeper into Jesus today. I fully open my life to you in every dimension and aspect—my body, my soul, and my spirit—choosing to be filled with you, to walk in step with you in all things. Apply to me, blessed Holy Spirit, all of the work and all of the gifts in pentecost. Fill me afresh, blessed Holy Spirit. I receive you with thanks and give you total claim to my life (and my wife and/or children).

Heavenly Father, thank you for granting to me every spiritual blessing in the heavenlies in Christ Jesus.

I receive those blessings into my life today, and I ask the Holy Spirit to bring all those blessings into my life this day. Thank you for the blood of Jesus. Wash me once more with his blood from every sin and stain and evil device. I put on your armor—the belt of truth, the breastplate of righteousness, the shoes of the readiness of the gospel of peace, the helmet of salvation. I take up the shield of faith and the sword of the Spirit, the Word of God, and I wield these weapons against the Evil One in the power of God. I choose to pray at all times in the Spirit, to be strong in you, Lord, and in your might.

Father, thank you for your angels. I summon them in the authority of Jesus Christ and release them to war for me and my household. May they guard me at all times this day. Thank you for those who pray for me; I confess I need their prayers, and I ask you to send forth your Spirit and rouse them, unite them, raising up the full canopy of prayer and intercession for me. I call forth the kingdom of the Lord Jesus Christ this day throughout my home, my family, my life, and my domain. I pray all of this in the name of Jesus Christ, with all glory and honor and thanks to him.

Acknowledgments

My love and thanks to Travis, to Sealy and his team, to my allies at Thomas Nelson, to my friends at Ransomed Heart, to Jenny, and to my family. We did it.

DARE WE DESIRE?

But for real proof you must look at your own longings and
aspirations; you must listen to the deep themes of your own
life story.

—GERALD MAY

Longing is the heart's treasury.

—AUGUSTINE

What do you want?

—JESUS OF NAZARETH

The shriveled figure lay in the sun like a pile of rags dumped there
by accident. It hardly appeared to be human. But those who used
the gate to go in and out of Jerusalem recognized him. It was his
spot and had been for as long as anyone could remember. He was
disabled, dropped off there every morning by someone in his family, and picked up again at the end of the day. Over the years, a
sort of gallery of human brokenness gathered by the pool of
Bethesda—the lame, the blind, the deaf, lepers, you name it. A
rumor was going around that sometimes (no one really knew when)
an angel would stir the waters, and the first one in would be healed.
Sort of a lottery, if you will. And as with every lottery, the desperate

gathered round, hoping for a miracle. So—technically speaking—
the man was never alone. But it had been so long since anyone had
actually spoken to him, he thought the question was meant for
someone else. Squinting upward into the sun, he didn't recognize
the figure standing above him. The misshapen man asked the fellow to repeat himself; perhaps he had misheard. Although the voice
was kind, the question felt harsh, even cruel.

"Do you want to get well?"

He sat speechless, blinking into the sun. Slowly, the words
seeped into his consciousness, like a voice calling him out of a
dream. Do I want to get well? Slowly, like a wheel long rusted, his
mind began to turn over. What kind of question is that? Why else
would I be lying here? Why else would I have spent every day for
the past thirty-eight seasons lying here? He is mocking me. The
man was familiar with mockery and had endured his share of
ridicule. But now that his vision had adjusted to the glare, he could
see the inquisitor's face, his eyes. There was no hint of mockery.
The face was as kind as the voice he heard. Apparently, the man
meant what he said, and he was waiting for an answer. "Do you
want to get well? What is it that you want?"

"Hey, there, you without the legs—what are you lying here for?
Wouldn't you love to get up, stretch yourself a bit, have a walk
around?" Who dared ask something so callous? It was Jesus who
posed the question, so there must be something we're missing here.
He is love incarnate. Why did he ask the paraplegic such an embarrassing question? Of course the fellow wanted to get well. You don't
have to be God to see the obvious. Or was it? As with most of the
questions he posed, Jesus was probing for something we do not see.
He knew the answer, of course—but did the man? Do we? Think
of the fellow on the ground for a moment; put yourself, literally, in
his shoes. His entire life has been shaped by his brokenness. All his
days he has wanted one thing. Forget riches. Forget fame. Life for

this man was captured in one simple, unreachable desire. When the other children ran and played, he sat and watched. When his family stood at the temple to pray, he lay on the ground. Every time he needed to have a drink or to go to the bathroom, someone had to pick him up and take him there.

So he had gone there for the past thirty-eight years, hoping to hit the jackpot. Sure, it was a long shot, but it was all he had. At what point did he begin to lose hope? First a year, then two went by. Nothing, at least for him. Maybe someone else got a miracle; that would buy him some time. What about after five years with no results? Ten? How long can we sustain desire against continual disappointment? Some hold out longer than others, but eventually, we all move to a place of resignation or cynicism or bitterness. As the years rolled on, this man, like all of us, began to lose any vital heart-connection to what he wanted. He was present, but not accounted for. The calluses had formed—not in the heart of Jesus, but over the man's heart. He had abandoned desire. Jesus took him back into the secret of his own heart. By asking him what he wanted, Jesus took the man back into his desire. Why?

It is where we must go if we are to meet God.

AN INVITATION TO DESIRE

This may come as a surprise to you: Christianity is not an invitation to become a moral person. It is not a program for getting us in line or for reforming society. It has a powerful effect upon our lives, but when transformation comes, it is always the aftereffect of something else, something at the level of our hearts. At its core, Christianity begins with an invitation to desire. Look again at the way Jesus relates to people. As he did with the fellow at the Sheep Gate, he is continually taking them into their hearts, to their deepest desires.

The story of the two blind men on the road to Jericho repeats the theme. Jesus is passing by the spot where these two men have sat looking for a handout for who knows how long. They learn that Jesus is going by, and they cry out for him. Though the crowd tries to shut them up, they succeed in shouting over the ruckus and capturing the Master's attention. The parade stops. Jesus steps to the side of the road, and standing there before him are two men, nothing clearer than the fact that they are blind. "What do you want me to do for you?" Again the question. Again the obvious that must not be so obvious after all.

Then there is the Samaritan woman whom Jesus meets at the well. She has come alone in the heat of the day to draw water, and they both know why. By coming when the sun is high, she is less likely to run into anyone. You see, her sexual lifestyle has earned her a "reputation." Back in those days, having one partner after another wasn't looked so highly upon. She's on her sixth lover, and so she'd rather bear the scorching rays of the sun than face the searing words of the "decent" women of the town who come at evening to draw water. She succeeds in avoiding the women, but runs into God instead. What does he choose to talk to her about—her immorality? No, he speaks to her about her thirst: "If you knew the generosity of God and who I am, you would be asking me for a drink, and I would give you fresh, living water" (John 4:10 The Message). Remarkable. He doesn't give a little sermon about purity; he doesn't even mention it, except to say that he knows what her life has been like: "You've had five husbands, and the man you're living with now isn't even your husband" (John 4:18 The Message). In other words, now that we both know it, let's talk about your heart's real thirst, since the life you've chosen obviously isn't working. "The water I give will be an artesian spring within, gushing fountains of endless life" (John 4:14 The Message).

Later in the gospel of John, Jesus extends the offer to anyone who realizes that his life just isn't touching his deep desire: "If you are thirsty, come to me! If you believe in me, come and drink! For the Scriptures declare that rivers of living water will flow out from within" (John 7:37–38 NLT). His message wasn't something new, but it confounded the religious leaders of the day. Surely, those scripturally learned Jews must have recalled God's long-standing invitation to them, spoken seven hundred years earlier through the prophet Isaiah:

> Come, all you who are thirsty,
>> come to the waters;
> and you who have no money,
>> come, buy and eat!
> Come, buy wine and milk
>> without money and without cost.
> Why spend money on what is not bread,
>> and your labor on what does not satisfy?
> Listen, listen to me, and eat what is good,
>> and your soul will delight in the richest of fare.
>
> (Isa. 55:1–2 NIV)

Somehow, the message had gotten lost by the time Jesus showed up on the scene. The Jews of his day were practicing a very soul-killing spirituality, a lifeless religion of duty and obligation. They had abandoned desire and replaced it with knowledge and performance as the key to life. The synagogue was the place to go to learn how to get with the program. Desire was out of the question; duty was the path that people must walk. No wonder they feared Jesus. He came along and started appealing to desire.

To the weary, Jesus speaks of rest. To the lost, he speaks of finding your way. Again and again and again, Jesus takes people back to their desires: "Ask and it will be given to you; seek and you will find; knock and the door will be opened to you" (Matt. 7:7 NIV). These are outrageous words, provocative words. Ask, seek, knock— these words invite and arouse desire. What is it that you want? They fall on deaf ears if there is nothing you want, nothing you're looking for, nothing you're hungry enough to bang on a door over.

Jesus provokes desire; he awakens it; he heightens it. The religious watchdogs accuse him of heresy. He says, "Not at all. This is the invitation God has been sending all along." He continues,

> You have your heads in your Bibles constantly because you think you'll find eternal life there. But you miss the forest for the trees. These Scriptures are all about me! And here I am, standing right before you, and you aren't willing to receive from me the life you say you want. (John 5:39–40 The Message)

LIFE IN ALL ITS FULLNESS

Eternal life—we tend to think of it in terms of existence that never comes to an end. And the existence it seems to imply—a sort of religious experience in the sky—leaves us wondering if we would want it to go on forever. But Jesus is quite clear that when he speaks of eternal life, what he means is life that is absolutely wonderful and can never be diminished or stolen from you. He says, "I have come that they may have life, and have it to the full" (John 10:10 NIV). Not, "I have come to threaten you into line," or "I have come to exhaust you with a long list of demands." Not even, "I have come primarily to forgive you." But simply, My purpose is to bring you life in all its fullness. Dallas Willard writes in The Divine Conspiracy,

> Jesus offers himself as God's doorway into the life that is truly life. Confidence in him leads us today, as in other times, to

become his apprentices in eternal living. "Those who come through me will be safe," he said. "They will go in and out and find all they need. I have come into their world that they may have life, and life to the limit."

In other words, eternal life is not primarily duration but quality of life, "life to the limit." It cannot be stolen from us, and so it does go on. But the focus is on the life itself. "In him was life," the apostle John said of Jesus, "and that life was the light of men" (John 1:4 NIV). Notice that the people who aren't so good at keeping up with the program but who are very aware of their souls' deep thirst are captured by Jesus' message. Common folk tear the roofs off houses to get to him. They literally trample each other in an effort to get closer to this man. I've never seen anyone acting like this in order to get a chance to serve on some church committee or to hear a sermon on why dancing is "of the devil." People act like this when it's a matter of life and death. Crowds trample each other to get out of a burning building; they press into the mob to reach a food line. When life is at stake and the answer is within reach, that's when you see human desire unmasked in all its desperation.

The Pharisees miss the boat entirely. Their hearts are hardened by the very law they claimed would bring them life. They put their hope in rules and regulations, in knowing and doing things perfectly. Having killed their souls' thirst with duty, they went on to kill their souls' only Hope, thinking they were doing their duty.

GOOD NEWS THAT'S NOT REALLY

Things appear to have come full circle. The promise of life and the invitation to desire have again been lost beneath a pile of religious teachings that put the focus on knowledge and performance.

> History has brought us to the point where the Christian message is thought to be essentially concerned only with how to deal with sin: with wrongdoing or wrong-being and its effects. Life, our actual existence, is not included in what is now presented as the heart of the Christian message, or it is included only marginally. (The Divine Conspiracy)

Thus Willard describes the Gospels we have today as "gospels of sin management." Sin is the bottom line, and we have the cure. Typically, it is a system of knowledge or performance, or a mixture of both. Those in the knowledge camp put the emphasis on getting our doctrine in line. Right belief is seen as the means to life. Desire is irrelevant; content is what matters. But notice this—the Pharisees knew more about the Bible than most of us ever will, and it hardened their hearts. Knowledge just isn't all it's cracked up to be. If you are familiar with the biblical narrative, you will remember that there were two special trees in Eden—the Tree of Knowledge of Good and Evil and the Tree of Life. We got the wrong tree. We got knowledge, and it hasn't done us much good. T. S. Eliot lamented,

> Endless invention, endless experiment,
> Brings knowledge of motion, but not of stillness;
> Knowledge of speech, but not of silence;
> Knowledge of words, and ignorance of the Word.
> Where is the Life we have lost in living?
> Where is the wisdom we have lost in knowledge?
> ("Choruses from the Rock")

Christianity is often presented as essentially the transfer of a body of knowledge. We learn about where the Philistines were from, and how much a drachma would be worth today, and all sorts of things about the original Greek. The information presented could not seem more irrelevant to our deepest desires.

Then there are the systems aimed at getting our behavior in line, one way or another. Regardless of where you go to church, there is nearly always an unspoken list of what you shouldn't do (tailored to your denomination and culture, but typically rather long) and a list of what you may do (usually much shorter—mostly religious activity that seems totally unrelated to our deepest desires and leaves us only exhausted).

And this, we are told, is the good news. Know the right thing; do the right thing. This is life? When it doesn't strike us as something to get excited about, we feel we must not be spiritual enough. Perhaps once we have kept the list long enough, we will understand.

We don't need more facts, and we certainly don't need more things to do. We need Life, and we've been looking for it ever since we lost Paradise. Jesus appeals to our desire because he came to speak to it. When we abandon desire, we no longer hear or understand what he is saying. But we have returned to the message of the synagogue; we are preaching the law. And desire is the enemy. After all, desire is the single major hindrance to the goal—getting us in line. We are told to kill desire and call it sanctification. Or as Jesus put it to the Pharisees, "You load people down with rules and regulations, nearly breaking their backs, but never lift even a finger to help" (Luke 11:46 The Message). As a result, Willard says, "The souls of human beings are left to shrivel and die on the plains of life because they are not introduced into the environment for which they were made."

"I began to seriously question my faith," wrote a friend, "when I was suffering my second year of depression. People in church saw my depressed face, and they complimented me on how I was such a good Christian." I am not making this up. This poor fellow was actually cheered for doing well spiritually when it became apparent his soul was dying. "I thought the best way for a person to live is to keep his desires to a minimum so that he will be prepared to serve God." Isn't that the message? It may not be explicit (what we truly believe rarely is), but it's clear enough. Get rid of desire, and get with the program.

Compare the shriveled life held up as a model of Christian maturity with the life revealed in the book of Psalms:

> You have made known to me the path of life;
>> you will fill me with joy in your presence,
>> with eternal pleasures at your right hand.
>>> (16:11 NIV)

> As the deer pants for streams of water,
>> so my soul pants for you, O God.
> My soul thirsts for God, for the living God.
>> When can I go and meet with God?
>>> (42:1–2 NIV)

> O God, you are my God,
>> earnestly I seek you;
> My soul thirsts for you,
>> my body longs for you,
> in a dry and weary land,
>> where there is no water.
>>> (63:1 NIV)

Ask yourself, Could this person be promoted to a position of leadership in my church? Heavens, no. He is far too unstable, too passionate, too desirous. It's all about pleasure and desire and thirst. And David, who wrote most of the psalms, was called by God a "man after his own heart" (1 Sam. 13:14 NIV).

Christianity has nothing to say to the person who is completely happy with the way things are. Its message is for those who hunger and thirst—for those who desire life as it was meant to be. Why does Jesus appeal to desire? Because it is essential to his goal: bringing us life. He heals the fellow at the pool of Bethesda, by the way. The two blind men get their sight, and the woman at the well finds the love she has been seeking. Reflecting on these events, the apostle John looked at what Jesus offered and what he delivered and said, "He who has the Son has life" (1 John 5:12 NIV).

THE STORY OF DESIRE

We misunderstand the good news Jesus announced when we hear it outside the story God is telling. Good news, a report that brings us relief and joy at the same time, is news that speaks to our dilemma. Hearing from your doctor that the lump is benign is good news. Receiving a notice from the IRS that you will not be audited after all is good news. Getting a call from the police to say that they've found your daughter is good news. Being offered tips and techniques for living a more dutiful life isn't even in the field of good news. We know in our hearts that our dilemma cannot be, "I sure wish I could be a more decent chap. What I really need is a program to improve my morals." Now, Jesus seemed to think that what he was offering really and truly spoke to our dilemma. Those who grasped what he was saying agreed. So what is our dilemma? What do we need most desperately to hear? Where are we in the story?

Let us ask the storytellers. In many ways, Hollywood has mastered the art of speaking to the human predicament. Consider the success of James Cameron's 1997 film Titanic. Not only did it sweep the Oscars, but the movie has become the all-time leading box office hit, passing even Gone with the Wind. Ticket sales have reached nearly $2 billion. I know people who have seen it not once or twice, but multiple times. It is a phenomenon whose appeal surpassed generational and cultural boundaries. Why? Christian critiques of the film missed the mark entirely, focusing almost exclusively on moral issues (sin management brought to film review). I cannot help thinking that if those reviewers were at the well when the Samaritan woman came by, they would have given her an earful.

But much more is going on here. Obviously, the film touched a nerve; it tapped into the reservoir of human longing for life. What is its story line? The film begins with romance, a story of passionate love, set within an exciting journey. Those who saw Titanic will recall the scene early in the film where the two lovers are standing on the prow of the great ship as it slices through a golden sea into a luscious sunset. Romance, beauty, adventure. Eden. The life we've all been searching for because it's the life we all were made for. Have we forgotten—or never been told? Once upon a time, in the beginning of humanity's sojourn on earth, we lived in a garden that was exotic and lush, inviting and full of adventure. It was "the environment for which we were made," as the sea lion was made for the sea. Now, those of you who learned about Eden in Sunday school maybe missed something here. Using flannel graphs to depict Paradise somehow doesn't do it. Picture Maui at sunset with your dearest love. A world of intimacy and beauty and adventure.

But then tragedy strikes. I'm sure I won't ruin the story for anyone if I tell you the ship goes down. How awful, how haunting are those scenes of the slow but irreversible plunge of the great ocean liner, leaving behind a sea of humanity to freeze to death in the Arctic waters. Everything is gone—the beauty, the romance, the adventure. Paradise is lost. And we know it. More than ever before, we know it. There was a time earlier in this century when we believed in the future, in something called progress. Not anymore, especially not the younger generations. I have yet to meet a young person who believes that his life will be better in a few years. As Chesterton said, we all somehow know that we are the "survivors of a wreck, the crew of a golden ship that had gone down before the beginning of the world." The ship has gone down. We are all adrift in the water, hoping to find some wreckage to crawl upon to save ourselves.

But that is not all. The secret of the film's success is found in the final scene. As the camera takes us once more to the bottom of the sea and we are given a last look at the rotting hulk of the once great ship, something happens. The Titanic begins to transform before our eyes. Light floods in through the windows. The rust and decay melt away as the pristine beauty of the ship is restored. The doors fly open, and there are all the great hearts of the story, not dead at all, but quite alive and rejoicing. A party is under way; a wedding party. The heroine, dressed in a beautiful white gown, ascends the staircase into the embrace of her lover. Everything is restored. Tragedy does not have the final word. Somehow, beyond all hope, Paradise has been regained.

Isn't this our dilemma? Isn't this the news we have been longing for? A return of the life we prize? Look again at what Jesus offers. There is bread enough for everyone. There is healing for every brokenness. The lost are found. The weary are given rest. There is life available—life to the limit.

> I am the Gate. Anyone who goes through me will be cared for—
> will freely go in and out, and find pasture. A thief is only there to
> steal and kill and destroy. I came so they can have real and eternal
> life, more and better life than they ever dreamed of. (John 10:9–10
> The Message)

DESIRE AND GOODNESS

But doesn't Christianity condemn desire—the Puritans and all that? Not at all. Quite the contrary. Christianity takes desire seriously, far more seriously than the Stoic or the mere hedonist. Christianity refuses to budge from the fact that man was made for pleasure, that his beginning and his end is a paradise, and that the goal of living is to find Life. Jesus knows the dilemma of desire, and he speaks to it in nearly everything he says.

When it comes to the moral question, it is not simply whether we say yes or no to desire, but always what we do with desire. Christianity recognizes that we have desire gone mad within us. But it does not seek to rectify the problem by killing desire; rather, it seeks the healing of desire, just as it seeks the healing of every other part of our human being.

"Two things contribute to our sanctification," wrote Pascal. "Pains and pleasures." And while we know that our journey is strewn with danger and difficulty, "the difficulties they meet with are not without pleasure, and cannot be overcome without pleasure." Where do you find Jesus saying, "The problem with you people is, you want too much. If you'd just learn to be happy with less, we'd all get along just fine"? Not anywhere. Quite the contrary. "My commands are for your good," he says, "always."

Something has gone wrong in us, very wrong indeed. So wrong that we have to be told that joy is found not in having another man's wife, but in having our own. But the point is not the law; the point is the joy. Need I say more than this: modern Christianity has brought an entire group of people to the point where they have to be told that sex is, in the words of one book, "intended for pleasure."

God is realistic. He knows that ecstasy is not an option; we are made for bliss, and we must have it, one way or another. He also knows that happiness is fragile and rests upon a foundation greater than happiness. All the Christian disciplines were formulated at one time or another in an attempt to heal desire's waywardness and so, by means of obedience, bring us home to bliss. Walter Brueggemann suggests that faith on its way to maturity moves from "duty to delight." If it is not moving, then it has become stagnant. If it has changed the goal from delight to duty, it has gone backward; it is regressing. This is the great lost truth of the Christian faith, that correction of Judaism made by Jesus and passed on to us: the goal of morality is not morality—it is ecstasy. You are intended for pleasure!

WHO, THEN, CAN BE SAVED?

Look again at the story Jesus told about the prodigal son. It might be called the story of desire. Consider what each character does with his desire. You have the younger son, whose desires get him into a world of trouble. Then there is the father, whose desire for the lost boy is so deep that he sees him coming from a long way off—he has been watching, waiting. Forgiveness is assumed; it's a given. He's grateful just to have the boy home again. And then there is the older brother. He's the party pooper, if you recall. His younger brother is "back from the dead," as the father says, and the older brother won't even come in for the celebration. He stands outside, sulking. Let's pick up the story there:

> The older brother was angry and wouldn't go in. His father came out and begged him, but he replied, "All these years I've worked hard for you and never once refused to do a single thing you told me to. And in all that time you never gave me even one young goat for a feast with my friends. Yet when this son of yours comes back after squandering your money on prostitutes, you celebrate by killing the finest calf we have." His father said to him, "Look, dear son, you and I are very close, and everything I have is yours. We had to celebrate this happy day. For your brother was dead and has come back to life! He was lost, but now he is found!" (Luke 15:28–32 NLT)

The older brother is the picture of the man who has lived his entire life from duty and obligation. When the wayward son returns from his shipwreck of desire, his brother is furious because he gets a party and not a trip behind the barn with the broadside of a paddle. He tells his father that he has been had; that all these years he hasn't gotten a thing in return for his life of service. The father's reply cuts to the chase: "All that is mine has always been yours." In other words, "You never asked." Rembrandt captures all this powerfully in his now-famous painting The Return of the Prodigal Son. In the painting, the elder brother stands a step above the reunion of father and son. He will not step down, enter in. He is above it all. But who receives redemption? The scandalous message of the story is this: those who kill desire—the legalists, the dutiful—are not the ones who experience the father's embrace. The question is not, Dare we desire, but dare we not desire?

ABOUT THE AUTHOR

JOHN ELDREDGE is the founder and director of Ransomed Heart™ Ministries in Colorado Springs, Colorado, a fellowship devoted to helping people recover and live from their deep heart. John is the author of numerous books, including *Waking the Dead, Wild at Heart, The Sacred Romance*, and *The Journey of Desire*. John lives in Colorado with his wife, Stasi, and their three sons, Samuel, Blaine, and Luke. He is an avid outdoorsman who loves being in the wild.

To learn more about John's seminars, audiotapes, and other resources for the heart, visit him on the Web at:

www.RansomedHeart.com

Or, write:

Ransomed Heart™ Ministries
P.O. Box 51065
Colorado Springs, CO 80949-1065

WAKING THE DEAD:
THE GLORY OF A HEART FULLY ALIVE

In *Waking the Dead,* John Eldredge shows us how God restores our hearts, our true humanity, and sets us free. There are four streams, Eldredge says, through which we can discover the abundant life: Walking with God, Receiving God's Intimate Counsel, Deep Restoration, and Spiritual Warfare. And once the "eyes of our hearts" are opened, we will embrace three eternal truths: Things are not what they seem; This is a world at war; Each of us has a crucial role to play. A battle is raging. And it is a battle for your heart.

Other Editions
Abridged Audio in 3 CDs—ISBN 0-7852-6299-7

COMING NOVEMBER 2003

A GUIDEBOOK TO WAKING THE DEAD:
EMBRACING THE LIFE GOD HAS FOR YOU
(John Eldredge and Craig McConnell)

ISBN 0-7852-6309-8

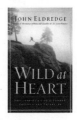

Every man was once a boy. And every little boy has dreams, big dreams. But what happens to those dreams when they grow up? In *Wild at Heart,* John Eldredge invites men to recover their masculine heart, defined in the image of a passionate God. And he invites women to discover the secret of a man's soul and to delight in the strength and wildness men were created to offer.

Hardcover Edition—ISBN 0-7852-6883-9
Abridged Audio in 3 CDs—ISBN 0-7852-6298-9
Abridged Audio in 2 Cassettes—ISBN 0-7852-6498-1

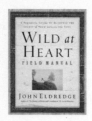

Abandoning the format of workbooks-as-you-know-them, the *Wild at Heart Field Manual* will take you on a journey through which John Eldredge gives you permission to be what God designed you to be—dangerous, passionate, alive, and free. Filled with questions, exercises, personal stories from readers, wide-open writing spaces to record your "field notes," this book will lead you on a journey to discover the masculine heart that God gave you.

ISBN 0-7852-6574-0

WILD AT HEART: A BAND OF BROTHERS

Five friends. Eight days. No scripts. Here's what it looks like to live the message of *Wild at Heart* in a band of real brothers. John and his band of brothers spent eight days shooting this series on a ranch in Colorado. Horses. Rappelling. White-water rafting. Fly-fishing. And some of the most honest conversation you will ever hear from men. This is not a scripted instructional video. It is real life and conversation shared with the cameras rolling. If you're looking for more, this is the next step in the *Wild at Heart* adventure for you and your band of brothers. The Multi-Media Facilitator's Kit includes John's bestselling *Wild at Heart* hardcover book; the *Wild at Heart Field Manual;* the *Wild at Heart Facilitator's Guide;* the video teaching series available either in VHS or DVD format; and a media kit to help you get the word out about joining a band of brothers.

ISBN 0-7852-6278-3

COMING NOVEMBER 2003

The Wild at Heart Journal is a leatherbound guided journey to help men explore their hearts and journal their adventures. This includes totally different material than that found in the *Field Manual.*

ISBN 0-8499-5763-X

Author Dan Allender calls *The Journey of Desire* "a profound and winsome call to walk into the heart of God." This life-changing book picks up where *The Sacred Romance* leaves off and continues the journey. In it, John Eldredge invites you to abandon resignation, to rediscover your God-given desires, and to search again for the life you once dreamed of.

Hardcover Edition—ISBN 0-7852-6882-0
Trade Paper Edition—ISBN 0-7852-6716-6

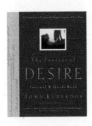

In *The Journey of Desire Journal and Guidebook,* John Eldredge, with Craig McConnell, offers a unique, thought-provoking, and life-recapturing workbook that invites you to rediscover your God-given desire and to search again for the life you once dreamed of. Less of a workbook and more of a flowing journal, this book includes personal responses to questions from John and Craig.

ISBN 0-7852-6640-2

The Sacred Romance (Brent Curtis and John Eldredge). This life-changing book has guided hundreds of thousands of readers from a busyness-based religion to a deeply felt relationship with the God who woos you. As you draw closer to him, you must choose to let go of other "less-wild lovers," such as perfectionistic drivenness and self-indulgence, and embark on your own journey to recover the lost life of your heart and with it the intimacy, beauty, and adventure of life with God.

Trade Paper Edition—ISBN 0-7852-7342-5
Special Collector's Edition (Hardcover)—ISBN 0-7852-6723-9
Abridged Audio in 2 cassettes—ISBN 0-7852-6786-7
Spanish Edition—ISBN 0-8811-3648-4

The Sacred Romance Workbook and Journal is a guided journey of the heart featuring exercises, journaling, and the arts to usher you into an *experience*—the recovery of your heart and the discovery of your life as part of God's great romance.

ISBN 0-7852-6846-4

The Three Classics: *The Sacred Romance, The Journey of Desire,* and *Wild at Heart.* Whether this special set is for yourself, to replace the dog-eared and penciled-in copies you already own, or a gift to share John's powerful message with someone you love, these Three Classics from John Eldredge will continue to give long after they are received.

ISBN 0-7852-6635-6

Dare to Desire, complete with beautiful, full-color design, is the perfect book if you are ready to move beyond the daily grind to a life overflowing with adventure, beauty, and a God who loves you more passionately than you dared imagine. With brand-new content as well as concepts from *The Sacred Romance, The Journey of Desire,* and *Wild at Heart,* John Eldredge takes you on a majestic journey through the uncharted waters of the human heart.

ISBN 0-8499-9591-4